CW01080229

THE ASHRIDGE GUIDE TO SELF-MANAGED DEVELOPMENT

THE ASHRIDGE GUIDE TO SELF-MANAGED DEVELOPMENT

An exclusive edition for Ashridge programme participants

FIONA ELSA DENT
ROBERT A. MACGREGOR
STEFAN WILLS

FINANCIAL TIMES

PITMAN PUBLISHING

PITMAN PUBLISHING

128 Long Acre, London WC2E 9AN

A Division of Longman Group Limited

First published as *Signposts for Success* by
Financial Times/Pitman Publishing, 1994

British Library Cataloguing in Publication Data
A CIP catalogue record for this book can be obtained from the British Library.

ISBN 0 273 61325 1

1 3 5 7 9 10 8 6 4 2

Typeset and illustrated by PanTek Arts, Maidstone, Kent
Printed and bound in Great Britain by
Biddles Ltd, Guildford and King's Lynn.

The Publishers' policy is to use paper manufactured
from sustainable forests.

*Ashridge is a charity number 311096 registered as
Ashridge (Bonar Law Memorial) Trust*

CONTENTS

Stage 3
TRAVELLING THE WAY   153

MESSAGE FROM THE DEAN

Firstly, I would like to extend my personal good wishes to you on completion of your executive development programme at Ashridge.

I sincerely hope that you have enjoyed being part of the Ashridge learning culture, albeit for a short period of time.

A residential programme at Ashridge presents a unique opportunity to look back and reflect on your past experience and to develop new approaches that will enable you to improve both your own personal performance and that of your organization.

Yet, I hope too that you will not see the programme simply as a 'one-off' development experience, but more as a launch pad for your further personal development. At Ashridge our underlying philosophy to management development is to interweave 'learning' and 'doing' so closely that we encourage you to take responsibility for your continued development when back at work.

Ashridge offers a number of innovative services and learning resources designed to support your self-development, some of which are described in the following pages.

In the meantime, I hope you will accept this practical workbook, written by an Ashridge faculty team, as a gift from Ashridge to help you get started on the journey. It will, I am sure, help you map out a route for yourself that will lead to a constantly enriching process of self-discovery and development.

I wish you every success for the future.

Peter J. Beddowes
Dean

THE ASHRIDGE GUIDE TO SELF-MANAGED DEVELOPMENT

A growing number of organizations in the 1990s now realize that it makes sense to encourage their people to examine their own strengths and areas for improvement. Rather than having their own development mapped out for them, managers are increasingly managing it themselves.

As a manager, you may feel energized by this freedom, and relish the challenge of undertaking your own development journey. Yet, as with any expedition, preparing and starting out is often the most difficult bit. Companies have a responsibility here: they cannot just leave you to decide on your own direction and somehow come back suitably enriched and experienced. You need, want and deserve structured support in planning out your personal itinerary and in sharing and testing out ideas. In many cases you may need help in learning *how* to learn.

Ashridge, with years of experience in executive development and an internationally expert facility and research base, is ideally positioned to guide and help managers in directing their self-development. Working with some of the world's leading organizations, we have learned ourselves exactly what managers want and need to manage their own development.

Ashridge now offers a portfolio of three self-development services, each of which answers the particular requirements of different groups of managers, complemented by a wealth of resources purpose-designed to support individual learning. Here we give an overview of these development experiences and resources, showing how you can direct and pursue your own development path in line with the current and future demands of your job.

For further details about these particular activities, or the full range of Ashridge's services in executive development, consultancy and research, please contact:

Ashridge Information Desk
Ashridge Management College
Berkhamsted
Herts HP4 1NS
England

Tel: +44 (0) 1442 843491
Fax: +44 (0) 1442 841209

THE ASHRIDGE SELF-MANAGED DEVELOPMENT WORKSHOP

Self-managed development [SMD] can be a great idea, providing people know where they're going and feel happy about it. When I got the team together to design the workshop, we had this image of a journey – a learning journey – in our minds. Our job is to point managers in the right direction, like navigators. After all, it's up to individuals to drive themselves forward, though I think the SMD Workshop is a very personally satisfying way of doing it. And if a company sends a group or team of managers together, it's also a cost-effective way for them to drive forward an organizational strategy. Fiona Dent, Programme Director

PARTICIPANT PROFILE

You are a manager who wishes to take increased responsibility for managing your own development. You may have a shrewd idea of the direction you wish to go in and require some self-development techniques and access to recources; or you may be at a threshold in your career development and wish to explore new options. Either way, you are keen to develop a plan for yourself in the future.

THE BENEFITS

You will

- increase your awareness of your own development needs
- acquire the tools, framework and techniques for managing your own development
- develop an action plan to get started.

THE APPROACH

You are asked to complete some diagnostic questionnaires before the workshop begins; the results are fed back to you at Ashridge, when there are opportunities for reflection and personal counselling. A self-managed development manual – specially prepared by the Ashridge programme design team – guides you as you explore a wide variety of issues which may help you to focus your development plan. Other features include short presentations, group discussions and group exercises. Nevertheless the emphasis is on you as an individual – you must be willing to take responsibility and control for exploring your own development needs.

COVERAGE

- introduction to self-managed learning
- the techniques and tools
- self-analysis
- developing learning relationships
- planning the way ahead.

KEY FACTS

Programme Director, Fiona Dent

| Duration: | three days |
| Venue: | Ashridge, England. |

Dates and fees on application.

IOC INTERNATIONAL EXECUTIVE DEVELOPMENT ALLIANCE

Offered by IOC-Ashridge (International Institute for Organizational Change, near Geneva)

Our discussions [...with a broad cross-section of international managers in different countries] showed us that managers wanted a development experience that would support them in their jobs. They say, "Hey, it's tough and chaotic out here, but if I'm going to achieve real results for the company I've got to keep getting better. And I want to develop at my own pace – in a way that suits my lifestyle best." So we got working and came up with the most flexible and wide-ranging individual development experience we could, but one that is truly "berufsbegleitend" – running in parallel to the job.
Claudia Heimer, IOC-Ashridge Research and Development Partner.

PARTICIPANT PROFILE

You are seeking a personalized development experience that is balanced with the demands of being an international executive. You understand the need to continue developing and review progress, although you probably feel that the types of development activity you would benefit from most are very varied and best approached over time.

THE BENEFITS

You will assess your personal needs in the light of your company's international business strategy and – with considerable expert support – plan, evolve and direct your own international career development experience tailored to your specific needs. You will have the opportunity to learn by networking, benchmarking and sharing the experiences of people from other organizations and countries.

THE APPROACH

The International Executive Development Alliance is a learning experience, paced over a year, which is anchored in a relationship with an IOC-

Ashridge 'learning partner' who is on hand to guide you and provide information and a reference point for your development. You follow your own individual learning 'map' within a flexible structure which includes these features.

- *Career development review*: an assessment of individual learning needs set in the context of research findings into the competences of successful international managers. This takes place as part of an initial three-day workshop at IOC, which also introduces the principles and techniques of self-managed development.
- *International learning relationships*: at this stage you may be seeking to build learning relationships with various people. They could be network contacts, role models, mentors or even mentees, either within or outside your organization.
- *Shadowing arrangements, international projects and international secondments* may all be additional options identified in your career development map, and which may create interesting and challenging experiences in other organizations and countries.
- In addition, Members of the Alliance meet together for three further one-day meetings at IOC to share experiences and to review and compare progress via experimental learning groups.

KEY FACTS

Programme Coordinator: Claudia Heimer

Choice of two intakes in Spring and Autumn of each year.

FEES

A membership fee of FF25000 includes participation in the initial three-day workshop and three further one-day meetings at IOC. Fees for individual support and development activities are charged separately at an appropriate rate agreed between the Alliance members and the sponsoring organization.

THE ASHRIDGE
SELF-DEVELOPMENT
SUMMER SCHOOL

When managers leave Ashridge after a programme, the most common feedback about our facilities and the Learning Resource Centre runs something like: "Marvellously equipped centre. Great leisure facilities. Lovely house and gardens. Shame I didn't have more time to use and appreciate it all.' So we thought, well, what about a first-class self-development experience that would give people the flexibility and opportunity to choose exactly how they spend their learning time? So the idea for the Summer School was born.'
Andrew Ettinger, Joint Programme Directon

PARTICIPANT PROFILE

You are a busy executive seeking to update your management learning and pursue your self-development in a relaxing environment with complete access to the full range of resources you require. In the past, you may have postponed attending business briefings or following up personal learning opportunities because of work commitments – you may therefore be seeking to combine such activities with a break from your place of work during the summer months. A special combined rate allows you to bring your partner for the week to participate in the full range of activities.

THE BENEFITS

You are able to:

- pursue your personal learning priorities using the wide-ranging resources available at Ashridge
- update your knowledge of topical management and business issues
- develop new skills
- reflect on your personal priorities and issues in Ashridge's peaceful, friendly environment
- have fun and relax.

THE APPROACH

On arrival at Ashridge, you have an opportunity to discuss and assess your management learning priorities. Once you have clarified your aims, you select the activities you want to pursue during your stay. Experienced Ashridge tutors are on hand to suggest suitable 'learning route maps' for you to follow.

You create your own balance of work and play by choosing from a wide-ranging 'menu' of activities which includes:

- Topical management briefings: e.g. on Business Process Re-engineering, the 'Learning Organization' or Time Management
- Skills workshops: e.g. media-handling skills, presentation skills, writing skills, software skills, using 'Windows'
- Outdoor management development exercises designed to help you develop further your team-building and communication skills using the outdoor environment
- Personal learning: spend as much time as you like in Ashridge's multi-media Learning Resource Centre (see page xvii)
- Fitness and relaxation: executive health seminars complement Ashridge's leisure facilities, including a swimming pool, jacuzzi, sauna, squash and tennis courts, croquet lawn, golf practice net and pitch-and-putt course
- Nature and culture: a range of events running parallel to the learning activities allows you and your partner to enjoy the historic house, gardens and surrounding woodlands.

KEY FACTS

Programme Directors: Andrew Ettinger and Fiona Dent

Duration: seven days
Venue: Ashridge, England.

Dates and fees on application.

THE ASHRIDGE LEARNING RESOURCE CENTRE

Pivotal to Ashridge's approach to self-development is the Learning Resource Centre. Probably the most advanced centre of its kind in Europe, it integrates traditional and state-of-the-art resources, housing library collections, information services, personal computing and media training facilities and self-managed learning packs.

In addition to supporting participants on Ashridge's range of executive development programmes, the Centre is used by organizations and individuals as an additional training and development resource to support their own in-company initiatives.

Many blue chip companies are discovering the enormous benefits of using this unrivalled facility. As an integral part of their self-development, individual managers can use the Centre to obtain valuable information on markets and competitors; groups of managers use it to work on self-development and project-based exercises, often as part of an in-company training or development programme; and training professionals use it to develop new materials and fresh ideas.

The special benefits to you are:

- access to a wide range of live management information from the Centre's multi-media resources
- user-friendly self-managed learning packs, specially prepared and updated by Ashridge tutors and researchers, which can be used to improve knowledge of topical management issues
- fast access and expert guidance in using the learning resources from friendly professional staff – on hand for some 90 hours per week
- the opportunity to develop new learning materials designed in partnership with Ashridge to cater specifically for your needs
- freedom to choose just how long you utlize the Centre – Ashridge's first-class residential facilities are available if your development session or module lasts more than one day.

Subscriptions to the Centre can be taken out on a daily basis or a corporate fixed-term basis. Alternatively training managers may just wish to utilize the resources as part of an in-house training programme.

Please contact Andrew Ettinger, Learning Resources Manager at Ashridge, on +44 (0) 1442 841156 for further details.

Stage 1

THE TRAVELLING CONCEPT

'Few things are impossible to diligence and skill...Great works are performed not by strength, but perseverance.'

SAMUEL JOHNSON

INTRODUCTION

Self-managed development is not a new idea but certainly one that is beginning to catch on in a big way. The current organizational trend towards giving people more responsibility for their own working lives is beginning to have a major impact on organizations and their approach to managing and developing individuals.

In the past there was a tendency for individuals and their bosses to assume that the organization was responsible for training and development and that it would provide all staff with any training necessary for them to be effective in their job. So, what happened each year? The Training Manager would come along with a menu of training programmes, and places would be allocated according to identified needs. While programmes very often satisfied much of the need and still do to a large extent, the current movement towards 'more from less', multi-skilling and the all-round manager means that people are beginning to explore different avenues to meet their development needs.

This does not mean that organizations are shirking their responsibilities for the development of their people, rather they are encouraging them to take a more active role in the whole process. There is also a movement away from thinking that a training programme solves all your developmental needs. Many other avenues are open to both organizations and individuals. Some of these methods will be explored later in the book, see 'The structure of this book' (p.5).

The principle of self-managed development has been explored in detail by many writers and developers. However, in our experience, the problems for many individuals have been getting started and then focusing on the right issues. This book is designed to encourage you to take responsibility for your own development and especially to help you get started.

HOW THE BOOK WORKS

Our firm belief is that self-managed development is an interactive process. This book has been designed to provide you with the opportunity to begin that process – what this means is *it is meant to be written in and on*. We would also encourage you to talk and share with others your thoughts, ideas and plans.

This interactive process enables you to take part in various exercises and activities designed to analyse, review and plan your development. We have used a variety of different approaches including questionnaires, short exercises and activities, and we have also given examples and case studies, all of which are designed to help you think about your own current development and move towards having a clear focus for future development.

As you flick through this book you will find that some parts of it are more appealing to you than others. Indeed this is what we expect and is very much in keeping with our philosophy on self-managed development. You have the choice and the responsibility for what, when, and how, you do this. The motivation, of course, may come not only from within yourself but from:

- other aspects of your life
- other people
- the variety of life situations in which you find yourself.

The important things are that you:

- are aware of the wide variety of opportunities available to you
- have a clear focus on where you wish to go

● take control of and responsibility for your self-managed development.

We give suggestions about routes through the book later in this stage and before each milestone, but we also stress that it is you who will create the best journey for yourself. Advice and guidance along the way from others is part of the whole process, but only a part.

This is probably not a book to be read from beginning to end, nor is it a book to read once and put away. It is a bit like a favourite record – to be played and replayed when you are in the mood. It could also be likened to improving at a game or sport. For instance, when you first learn to ski you learn about the necessary equipment and familiarize yourself with the basics before you tackle even one of the easiest nursery slopes. Then, over a period of time, and with practice, you progress, to become more proficient and tackle more difficult runs.

For us, self-managed development is a bit like this. First you have to familiarize yourself with yourself, then you have to plan where you want to go next and how you are going to get there. The process is one of constantly reviewing and adding to your knowledge and skill – a bit like a never-ending journey, but in this case one with discovery along the way.

THE STRUCTURE OF THIS BOOK

This book is split into three main stages with milestones along the way.

Stage 1 – The travelling concept

This is the introductory phase which examines and explores our ideas about self-managed development and what it might involve for you.

Stage 2 – Preparing the way

This is the key element in our book and is all about 'getting you started'. It involves you in the self-managed development processes of analysis, review and planning. Its aim is to raise your own self-awareness to enable you to prepare fully for the journey ahead. Thorough preparation is so often the secret of success and in our view will certainly help you to focus on your self-managed development objectives. The four sub-sections are:

- Who am I?
- What have I done?
- How did I learn it?
- Where am I going?

All encourage you to examine yourself from a variety of perspectives.

Our ideas are supported by examples and case studies with exercises for you to complete to help you to focus on 'where you are going'.

Stage 3 – Travelling the way

This final stage in the book encourages you to begin action, planning and thinking about how you will travel the way ahead. We examine a variety of approaches to action planning as well as considering contingency plans and coping strategies for when things do not go to plan. Finally we make suggestions on keeping track of your self-managed development plans.

By this stage we hope that you are now excited by the opportunity to take more control of your own development. Here we examine some techniques for moving ahead. The key is that you recognize that it is your *own responsibility* – others can and will help along the way, but as someone once said 'your personal effectiveness is your own responsibility'.

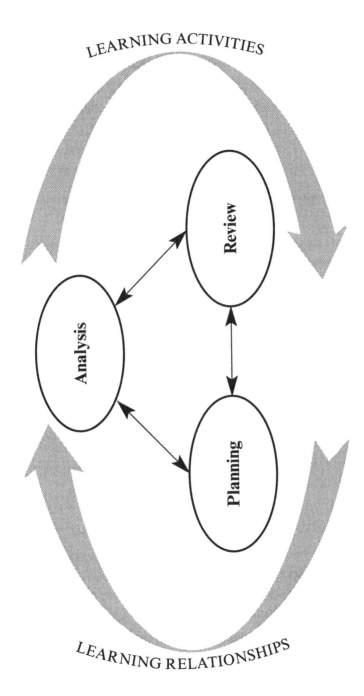

Fig 1.1 An interactive approach to self-managed development

WHAT IS SELF-MANAGED DEVELOPMENT?

'The people who get on in this world are the people who get up and look for the circumstances they want, and, if they can't find them, make them.'

GEORGE BERNARD SHAW

Quite simply, self-managed development is the process whereby you take responsibility and control for your own development – you may be motivated to do this for a variety of reasons. For instance:

- to manage your career more effectively
- to develop new skills or knowledge
- to improve your ability in your current job
- to manage a life change to greatest effect
- to be effective in a new project area.

By adopting a planned strategy for your development and by recognizing the wide variety of development opportunities available to you on a day-to-day basis, you can begin to make the most of everyday situations and turn many of them into personal developmental experiences.

Based on our experience of working with both individuals and organizations we have developed an approach which encompasses the important aspects of our way of doing things (Fig 1.1).

Our approach encompasses the three key stages in the interactive process of getting started on your own self-development. For many, self-analysis is the starting point, followed by a period of reflection and review. One could also call this thinking about ourselves, probably something we rarely do or have time to do. The output from this analysis and review process is a plan that not only helps you get started but helps you to focus along the way. There are two other important aspects to our approach: learning activities and learning relationships. Learning activities are the wide variety of experiences we have in life from which we can learn. The idea of a learning relationship is that even though we are concerned with self-managed development none of us learns in isolation. Throughout life we develop a variety of relationships many of which help us to learn and develop.

Below we examine each of the different parts of our approach in more detail, giving examples and ideas were appropriate.

OUR APPROACH EXPLAINED

We believe that there are five main processes that individuals are constantly involved in when managing their own development. We discuss them under the headings: analysis (p.9), review (p.13), planning (p.13), learning activities (p.16) and learning relationships (p.18). What follows is a description of each process and what it might involve.

Analysis

Analysis is any process that involves a method of assessing your current range of abilities/strengths/weaknesses/needs/wants/desires, etc.

Some common processes specifically designed to encourage you to analyse yourself are:

- assessment (at an assessment centre)
- performance appraisal/review/discussion
- completion of inventories/questionnaires.

Assessment (at an assessment centre)

Assessment may be used in the selection or development of individuals for specific roles in an organization. It is often used to identify management or 'high flier' potential and organizations regularly use assessments to select graduates on the 'milk round' (this is the name given to the selection process for current-year graduates taking up training positions in organizations). Typically at an assessment centre candidates will be given a variety of exercises to determine their abilities in a range of predetermined managerial competences. These exercises might include:

- questionnaires and inventories relating to critical reasoning, abilities and personality
- leaderless discussion groups
- business simulations
- one-to-one interviews with an assessor
- a business presentation.

Other key features of an assessment centre include the presence of a group of highly trained assessors, all of whom will be familiar with techniques being used and with the range of competences being measured. Following assessment at a centre each candidate should be debriefed in detail by one of the assessors about his or her performance. This can be a rich source of information regarding one's strengths and weaknesses and development needs.

Performance appraisal/reviews/discussion

Most individuals who work within an organization take part in some sort of performance appraisal scheme, usually on an annual basis. This typically involves completing a document covering:

- past performance
- objectives for the coming year
- career goals
- training and development needs.

The document is usually completed either during or after a discussion between the individual and the boss and thus forms the basis of that person's action plan for the year ahead. Increasingly organizations' performance appraisal systems are becoming more sophisticated and often involve a review of the competences necessary to be effective within the particular culture of the organization. In some ways the introduction of competence reviews makes this process even more relevant for self-managed development as the competence list can help you to identify specific areas for development (see Exercise 26 in the milestone 'What have I done?'). Again this can be a rich source of information regarding strengths and weaknesses and development needs.

Completion of inventories/questionnaires

Many of us complete an inventory or questionnaire during a selection process for a job or during a training programme. These are used for a wide variety of reasons. Many will be used to introduce frameworks and to examine preferences for aspects of the job role. For instance:

- the Belbin Team Type Inventory (BELBIN) examines your role preferences when working as part of a team
- the Myers Briggs Type Indicator (MBTI) is a personality inventory designed to help people understand themselves and their behaviours
- Fundamental Interpersonal Relationship Orientation Behaviour (FIRO – B) is a personality inventory designed to help people explore their interactions with other people
- an Occupational Personality Questionnaire (OPQ) indicates relevant personality characteristics across a wide spectrum of occupations
- the Thomas-Kilmann Conflict Mode Instrument indicates how people typically manage conflict.

None of these inventories measure ability in a specific area of work. Mostly they are designed to encourage individuals to become more self-aware and to help them explore aspects of managing relationships and behaviour. Often individuals complete these inventories and questionnaires to aid in the development process or as a discussion opener as part of a training programme or other development event. Typically they are used to assist in understanding certain aspects of an individual's approach to work or relationships, and possibly to highlight further development needs.

 Exercise 1

MY DEVELOPMENT EXPERIENCES

Note below the relevant experiences you have taken part in that have encouraged you to analyze your personal development needs.

Date	*Description of experience*
_____	_____
_____	_____
_____	_____
_____	_____
_____	_____
_____	_____

So, that is the analysis stage. Now let's move to another stage.

Review

A review is a form of evaluative process you take part in in order to reflect on information collected and to distil and make sense of data about your development. In fact it is thinking in a structured way about what the data is telling you.

Review can be based on historical data or on the here and now. It can be something you do on your own simply by thinking and perhaps asking yourself a range of thought-provoking questions such as:

- What are my current strengths?
- What are my weaknesses or development needs?
- How do these help me in my life at the moment?
- Where do I want to go now?
- What do I want to do next?
- What do I need to develop in order to get there?

A review can be something you do with the assistance of others. The important thing is that it is a reflective process where the outcome will be an improved sense of direction in terms of your future development needs. (Many of the exercises in this book are designed to help you to structure and organize your own self-knowledge.)

Planning

Planning involves asking yourself the following sorts of questions:

- How do I intend to meet my development needs?
- Why is it necessary to meet them?
- Where will I go to meet them?
- When will they have to be met?

It is often called action planning but in the context of self-managed development this involves choosing the most appropriate vehicle to satisfy your development needs. With this in mind it may often require you to plan how you are going to sell your idea or get permission for the methodology you choose. For instance, consider the following case:

Jane was a Branch Administrator for the Scottish Sales Division of a large insurance company. Her work had always been office-based, requiring her to act not only as a secretary to the sales staff but also as an intermediary going between the sales staff, the customers and Head Office. Over the years she had built up good relations with most of the customers and was highly regarded by both the sales staff and her boss as an efficient and effective operator.

She was very happy in her job and content to stay with it for a few more years. However, much of the job involved liaising with various departments at Head Office in Brighton. Sometimes both she and the sales staff experienced problems with this liaison: not so much with the people (though this could be a problem) but more with identifying the correct department to contact. Occasionally she met people from Head Office, either when they came to Scotland or when she attended Branch Administrators conferences , but she had never visited nor met most of the staff she dealt with on a day-to-day basis.

For some time she felt that she could add a new dimension to her job if she understood more about the machinations of working at Head Office and indeed she felt she could provide a more effective service to all her customers (sales staff, customers and Head Office contacts) if she knew more of the people personally, and understood more about the processes in which they were involved. In thinking through her plan she knew she would have to present a good case to her boss if she was to meet all her development needs.

When she eventually approached her boss she listed the key benefits that would result from her undertaking the exercise as follows:

Organizational benefits
- *Greater understanding of Head Office administrative procedures and processes leading to more efficient liaison between herself and Head Office*
- *Development of personal relationships between herself and Head Office staff leading to better working relationships in the future*
- *Possibility of building up a 'special' relationship between the Scottish office and Head Office along the lines of 'gosh they do care after all'*

Individual benefits
- *Improved knowledge of company systems leading to greater efficiency in her job*
- *Improved motivation brought about by her boss's investment in her development*
- *Fulfilment of her own personal need to get to know the full range of people she works with*
- *Possible future career development.*

Fortunately her planning paid off. The boss offered to take her down to Brighton on his next visit if she could present him with a plan of how she would spend her time during the two-day visit. She realized the hard work was only just beginning – she had to prove the investment was worth while.

Planning is therefore an active process whereby individuals think about where they wish to get to and how they are going to get there. It can be general or detailed, strategic or tactical, and may focus on short-, medium- or long-term arrangements. Exercises to help in the planning process are in the milestone 'Where am I going?' (p.131) and the final stage 'Travelling the way' (p.153).

These three processes form the basis of our approach to self-managed development and if you work through these stages then this will almost certainly help you get started. There are however two other important elements in our approach.

Learning activities

A learning activity is any event or experience either planned or spontaneous which provides you with the opportunity to develop.

As stated earlier, training programmes were often regarded as the major way of satisfying many development needs and indeed are often still a major part of many development processes. But over the past decade or so many other methods have become recognized as vehicles for satisfying development needs. In particular, with the growth of the concept of continuous learning, and learning through and on the job, many everyday experiences can be used as development opportunities. For instance:

- project work
- secondment
- job rotation
- coaching
- stretching new jobs
- new technology
- re-organization
- promotion
- chairing meetings.

For many of us, the issue is recognizing these sorts of experiences as potential learning and development activities and then focusing on how and what we can learn from the experience. This is why it is vital to have very clear objectives and plans to enable us to make the best of the learning opportunities that present themselves to us.

The following case study is a typical example of how one manager successfully overcame a weakness through using many of the principles of self-managed development.

Jim was 34 years of age. His job was as one of several Senior Finance Managers in his organization. He had been with the organization and in that position for three years. Throughout this time, and indeed through most of his career as an accountant, he had usually managed to avoid getting involved in giving formal presentations. It was an experience which terrified him – the few he had done were abysmal – and he was physically ill beforehand. He would shake during the presentation and as for the words and techniques he used, these left a lot to be desired. He had learned a long time ago that presenting was not for him. To get round the problem he would arrange either an informal roundtable discussion, or he would bring along a member of his team to do the bulk of the presentation, enabling him to take a back seat, only topping, tailing and chairing questions. He knew this was a fear many managers had, so until now felt he could get by with his coping strategy.

However, increasingly in his current job he was being pressurized to give formal presentations to the board and to customers. More importantly, he now wanted a change of job and knew that to move higher up the managerial ladder he would have to overcome his fear. Initially he sought out the advice of a trusted colleague in the Human Resources Division who suggested that a good starting point would be a short external workshop on Presentation Skills. He identified from a range of workshop outlines a three-day residential programme, that included lots of practice, focusing on the practicalities of giving presentations. Getting permission and finding the money to go presented him with no problem – he managed his own time anyway and his Training and Development budget was way underspent.

The same trusted colleague agreed to act as a coach on his return from the workshop to help him get the most from the experience and to further develop his skills. His plan from then on was to practise initially in relatively safe environments; for example, by giving more formal presentations as part of his regular weekly team briefings to his own staff, then giving short presentations to his peers and bosses at Finance Division meetings, with the eventual goal being a 20-minute slot at the Annual Sales Conference. He felt that while he was not the best performer at the sales conference he certainly was not the worst. Following the conference, and with the help of his 'coach', he reviewed what went well and what he needed to develop further. So, armed with his action plan, he continued his journey of improvement.

But what now? Jim is now the Finance Director of a large retail group. He regularly gives presentations to a wide range of audiences but he has never become blasé about his new-found confidence, recognizing that this is one skill he can always improve.

Jim's self-managed development plan involved:

- identifying a coach
- initiating a discussion with him
- identifying and attending a workshop
- getting feedback from his coach
- practising his approach in 'safe environments'
- a philosophy of continuous improvement.

Learning relationships

As can be seen from the example above, for many of us a vital part of our development involves creating and exploring relationships with others who can help us learn. A key relationship for those of us working in a company or in business might be with the organization. Self-managed development can be successful at an individual level without the commitment of the organization, but it is a much more powerful process if the organization actively encourages and supports people to take more responsibility for, and control of, their own development.

Organizations that actively encourage individuals in the process of self-managed development tend to find themselves with a more committed and motivated workforce. Clearly this approach is not without disadvantages and may pose new challenges for the organizational systems when people find more creative ways of satisfying their development needs than the traditional approaches that have been used in the past. In addition people may well grow more quickly and become more challenging and demanding in terms of career development and promotion. It seems to us that what the individual is seeking from his or her relationship with the organization is quite simply support and encouragement – though some may seek a more challenging relationship.

If systems are set in place, and clear objectives are agreed, then the process of self-managed development should present organizations with many advantages that will far outweigh the disadvantages. Apart from the key relationship with the organization, people will develop relationships with others. Many of you already have learning relationships with significant others but often you do not recognize them as such. Our definition of a learning relationship is 'any type of interaction which stimulates developmental activity'. Most individuals have well-developed networks within organizations and in other aspects of their lives. These networks provide you with many of the people needed for learning relationships.

Typically such people can come from a wide variety of sources:

- boss or manager
- peers or colleagues and other staff
- senior executives
- family
- social contacts and friends
- customers.

In defining the sorts of learning relationships you have with these people they can be one of several types. We believe that the primary relationships are between the individual and his or her:

- mentor
- coach
- counsellor
- role model
- fellow members of a learning support group.

A mentor

By mentor we mean someone who is an experienced and trusted adviser. Often an individual develops this type of relationship based on respect and admiration for that person's achievements. Ideally the person will combine excellent communication skills with the ability to listen effectively, challenge, support and guide without providing the answers. Rather they are a sounding board to whom an individual can go when they need someone to listen to them. A mentor does not have to be a boss; in fact it is usually a more successful relationship if the mentor has no professional responsibility for the individual. It is possible to have more than one mentor simultaneously, each perhaps helping us with a particular facet of our life; for instance one mentor for our role as people manager and another in our technical arena. Throughout life one may develop several different mentoring relationships. Here is a case study:

Jane was a young training officer when she met her first mentor, Bob, who was an older more experienced colleague, based at a different office. Bob provided Jane with a relationship based on mutual respect and understanding. He was a good listener, an even better questioner and very often challenged her and made her think at a very important time in her early career as a trainer. At the time Jane recognized that the relationship was a helping one but it is only now in thinking back that she realizes that Bob was probably her first real mentor.

In most of her jobs she has now identified people with whom she has developed similar relationships: people she regards as mentors for different parts of her career. She has found these relationships invaluable in helping her to grow and develop over the years as well as helping her to get over many sticky times.

 Exercise 2

MENTORS IN MY LIFE

Think back over your life so far. List down all the people who you would consider to have been mentors for you. State their relationship to you and describe what it involved.

_____

_____

_____

_____

_____

A coach

The coaching relationship is a helping relationship. Typically the coach will be a line manager or a specifically assigned individual who will help in some aspect of your development. The role of the coach can vary tremendously depending upon the stage of your development in a particular area. It differs from the mentoring relationship in one major way, and that is that the mentor will usually be someone who you select and with whom you develop a relationship; the coach will often be an assigned individual, or even your line manager. Many of the skills in the two roles however, are similar. Some organizations are now actively encouraging coaching as part of their managerial philosophy. This is also in line with the growing interest in self-managed development. So, while individuals take more control and responsibility for their own development the organization recognizes that this should not be in isolation and individuals will often require advice and guidance. The coaching role will provide this.

 Exercise 3

COACHES IN MY LIFE

Thinking back over your life so far, note down the people who have entered into coaching relationships with you and describe how they have helped you.

_____

_____

_____

_____

A counsellor

A counsellor is similar in some ways to a coach but does not necessarily provide training and development. A counsellor can be either *directive* or *non-directive*. By directive we mean the counsellor leads the dialogue. In non-directive counselling *you* lead the discussion. Counsellors tend to be used when the problem is of a more personal nature rather than a work-related issue. The counsellor is very often a trusted person who is a good listener and is discreet. Some organizations have systems set up to provide this service.

 Exercise 4

COUNSELLORS IN MY LIFE

Thinking back over your life so far, note down those people with whom you have had a counselling relationship. What did that relationship do for you and what skills did the counsellor have? You might find it useful to categorize these into 'directive' and 'non-directive' counselling relationships.

Directive   *Non-directive*

_____   _____

_____   _____

_____   _____

_____   _____

_____   _____

_____   _____

A role model

The role model differs again. It may well be someone you do not personally know (for instance, someone famous) or someone you know only by reputation or in passing (for instance, a senior colleague). Typically it could be someone you admire and who has reached a position in life to which you aspire. You may be attracted to some of his or her skills and attributes or simply just to the position and life or career experience. It could also be someone who manages a situation in a way that you would like to emulate.

 Exercise 5

ROLE MODELS IN MY LIFE

Thinking back over your life so far, list your role models and say why they were important for you.

_____

_____

_____

_____

_____

_____

Fellow members of a learning support group

This is a relatively new concept, and is sometimes an integral part of a training programme. Usually early on in the programme you are assigned to a small group and encouraged throughout the week to meet and share thoughts, ideas and problems. The primary aim is to help each other to learn and develop. Because they are specific to the course, it is unfortunate that these groups are usually disbanded at the end of a training programme as much useful work and effort in developing the group is lost. Fortunately in our lives both at work and outside work many of us are part of a network which fits the description of a learning support group. Are *you*?

Exercise 6

MY LEARNING SUPPORT GROUPS

Think about it; could you describe any of your networks as learning support groups? If so, list them below.

_____

_____

_____

_____

_____

Are there any networks to which you belong that could become learning support groups?

_____

_____

_____

_____

This now leads us to examine the bigger picture of the full range of our learning relationships. Having now reflected on the various relationships we have many of us may discover that we have quite a network of different ones.

The case study that follows is fairly typical of the sorts of examples we hear from many people with whom we have spoken.

Sally is Marketing Manager in a large multi-national company. She sees her boss – David, the director – as her coach. He provides her with challenges and opportunities, and guides her when necessary. She and her colleagues, the other Marketing Managers, act as supports for one another. They often meet both formally and informally to share ideas and problems.

She has one particular colleague (Sue), more experienced than she, with whom she spends more time. Sally regards her as a personal counsellor, with whom to share worries, problems and fears. Then there is Barry, her old friend. They share a special relationship. He is much older than Sally, successful and a great listener. He really is her mentor. He pulls no punches and has always been honest and fair in their discussions, guiding and helping, but not providing answers.

If we were to draw a 'learning relationship network' for Sally it might look like this:

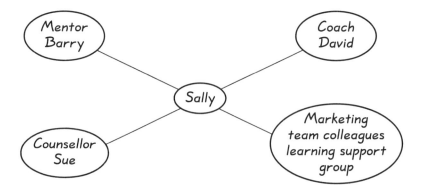

These are the people who are currently important to Sally in terms of her learning relationships. However this is not a static situation and we can expect people to enter and withdraw from the picture due to the ever-changing world in which we live.

Who would you currently include in your personal learning relationship network?

Exercise 7

MY LEARNING RELATIONSHIP NETWORK

Draw your own learning relationship network, first of all for how it is now, and then for how it has been over your life so far.

You might now like to bear these drawings in mind and link them to some of the exercises in 'Preparing the way' (p.31).

This completes our survey of the five elements of self-managed development (listed on p.9) that form the basis of our approach. These elements may be dealt with in any order. We hope that people will join the process where it is most appropriate for them and then move through the process at their own pace and in their own way.

For instance, you may recently have taken part in a training programme (*learning activity*) and on returning to work you are *reviewing* it with your boss. During this discussion you *analyse* which skills you have strengthened and which skills still require developing. This discussion prompts you to *plan* how you can continue to build on your strengths and develop strategies for lessening your weaknesses using everyday experiences as learning opportunities. This example illustrates how it is important to involve others in the process of self-managed development – as our diagram tries to illustrate. We believe that others can and should be involved in the process – *learning relationships.*

We hope that Stage 1 has introduced you to our practical ideas on managing your own development. In addition we hope you are becoming committed to the idea that 'your development is your responsibility'. Others can and will help you along the way but the more you take control and direct your energies the more rewarding and effective the process will be. This introductory phase has explored, and encouraged you to examine, the wide variety of resources available to you in this 'journey of discovery'. The next stage in the journey encourages you to delve deeper into yourself by exploring who you are, what you have done, how you learned and where you are going! The final stage asks you to plan the way ahead – always on the premise that this whole process is a journey not a destination.

SUMMARY OF KEY POINTS FOR STAGE 1

Looking back over the section 'What is self-managed development?' we have:

• Explained our approach to self-managed development by describing the five key elements, namely:

Analysis	the process of assessing your current range of abilities, strengths, weaknesses, needs, wants, desires
Review	an evaluative process to enable you to make sense of your development needs
Planning	an active process enabling you to choose and plan how to meet your needs
Learning activity	an event or experience providing you with the opportunity to develop
Learning Relationships	any type of interaction that stimulates developmental activity.

- Described each element with examples, cases and some introductory exercises.

Stage 2

PREPARING THE WAY

'You can only understand life backwards and yet we have to live it for-wards.'

SØREN KIERKEGAARD

INTRODUCTION

As we journey through life we all have the potential to learn and develop. For a host of reasons people are rarely able to reach their full potential. Some realize (or are in the process of realizing) most of their potential; others get around half-way; the rest hardly get off the starting blocks.

There are many complex individual and environmental factors why this is the case. Our experience suggests that a major reason why people differ is the increased pressure to be active and busy for as much of our waking hours as is practically possible. More than ever before we live in a society where to be doing things is generally thought of as being the most valued activity – particularly in our lives at work. The major drawback with this is that it leaves very little time to step back and reflect upon what we are doing – to reassess and ultimately to learn from our experiences and develop. This book is designed to help you to realize, and plan to meet, your potential.

In many spheres of life punctuating spells of hectic doing with periods of quiet reflection can be thought of as a rather self-indulgent way of life. Imagine the following scene:

A manager has his door closed, his feet on the desk and is staring into space reflecting on a recent incident. His manager walks in and is alarmed by what she sees. The reflecting manager sits up and proceeds to defend himself by arguing that he is trying to learn from an experience. Needless to say, his boss is not convinced!

One of our basic premises throughout this book is that if one is to learn and develop it is essential to create time to be able to reflect. 'Preparing the way' is all about taking the time to think about your life and career in order to give it greater meaning and direction. If it is to be thought of as a self-indulgent activity, then this section is all about you indulging yourself! We want to help you to indulge yourself so we have divided the section into four key milestones, each addressing a question aimed at encouraging you to reflect. They are:

- Who am I?
- What have I done?
- How did I learn it?
- Where am I going?

For people who are not used to spending time looking inward such reflection can be a difficult task. One of the best ways to overcome blockages of this kind is to start off with the broad context. Take a few minutes to construct your own general profile.

 Exercise 8

MY GENERAL PROFILE

What are the key words or phrases that best describe you as a person?

_____

_____

_____

In considering your life as a whole, what have you excelled at?

_____

_____

_____

What have you not excelled at?

_____

_____

_____

In terms of work, what do you like doing best?

_____

_____

_____

Similarly, what do you like doing least?

_____

_____

_____

How would you describe the people with whom you relate best?

_____

_____

_____

How would you describe the people with whom you find it difficult to relate?

_____

_____

_____

How would you like to develop and improve in the future?

_____

_____

_____

Remember that you have only just started and your thoughts/ideas could change over time. With this in mind don't be afraid to come back to this section (or any other for that matter) and have a second look.

You are now prepared and ready to start your journey – 'Bon Voyage!'

Who am I?

Here we encourage you to be as honest as you can in answering the question 'who am I?' We suggest a variety of different ways of looking at yourself in order to help you get a clear picture of yourself. We introduce a range of different approaches and exercises that help you to look back over your life. We regard them as techniques that will help you make sense of who you are in the context of self-managed development.

Anyone genuinely interested in self-managed learning and development will probably need to begin the process by demonstrating an appropriate level of self-awareness or knowledge. What is meant exactly by the term 'self-awareness?' At one extreme it is possible to answer the question 'who am I?' with details such as the following:

My name is Mick Jones.
I live at 5 Manor Road.
I have a wife and three children.
I work as a sales engineer.

Although such details might be extremely relevant in drawing together an overall picture of a person in this form they do not really tell us much about who Mick Jones is. Clearly in the context that we are using it self-awareness comes from observing, analyzing and reflecting on the sort of information which tells us something about Mick Jones' personality.

FOCUS ON YOUR PERSONALITY

Analysing who you are at this depth is not, and never will be, an exact science. The complexity of this analyzing is compounded by the fact that your personality is never completely static. It evolves through time from who you were (in the past) through who you are (right now) to who you will be (at some point in the future). Analysing such development is extremely dependent upon two major ingredients: you, and your learning relationships. You are the link point with the potential to bring it all together. To do this it is vital that you are able to build an accurate profile of yourself, based upon your past and present, before you journey into the far less certain realm of the future. In building this profile, you can draw upon a wide range of resources from the learning relationships in which you engage, to the wide variety of learning activities you undertake in your life.

You might also like to think of your personality as analogous to a section of coastline. Wherever one might look or explore no two sections are exactly the same. Extending the analogy further, coastline is continually subject to a weathering process which changes it slowly over time. Map-makers put grids over specific sections in attempts to plot the major features. This is precisely what this section is intended to achieve. Reflecting on and plotting the major features of your personality will go a long way towards helping you to gain a much clearer understanding of 'Who am I?'.

The extent to which this weathering process is different for all of us is most apparent in childhood. Consider the following story.

After being posted to a new job in Hong Kong a colleague of ours decided to go for a walk in a park. He noticed a friend walking ahead with her husband and small child. To his amazement the parents seemed to be behaving very strangely.

Periodically they would leave their child and hide behind a tree. When the child realized that his parents had disappeared he screamed, at which time the parents returned and reassured him. The next day our colleague quizzed his friend on what sort of game they were playing. 'It was not a game', his friend said rather abruptly. This is just the sort of practice many Chinese parents in Hong Kong undertake in order to make children realize firstly that they are part of a collective family and secondly that they need their family. This left our colleague reflecting on how this contrasted with his own society's tendency to encourage independence in its young.

So, the weathering process acts on all of us in different ways, producing different end results due to a multitude of individual differences. It cannot therefore be surprising that we are thought of as highly complex beings, notoriously difficult to understand. If this is so, can we ever really know the inner workings of ourselves

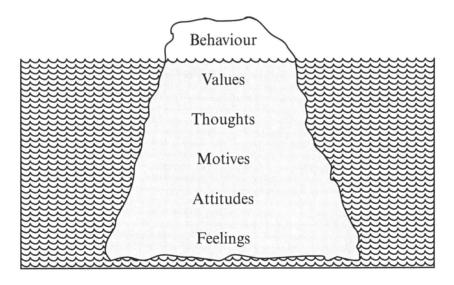

Fig 2.1 The iceberg

and others? Don't despair because it is possible to break down a complex object such as personality into distinct parts and then try to understand the whole object through its major features. As mentioned earlier it can never be an exact science – but breaking personality down into major parts is always helpful.

Another useful analogy in this context is that which compares who you are to an iceberg (Fig 2.1). A notable feature of an iceberg is that a small portion of it sticks out above the surface of the water for all the world to see. Much less obvious is the fact that the huge bulk of it stays hidden below the surface of the water. Your personality is similar – much of it stays hidden from the outside world. Your personality often affects how you see yourself, and can be useful in understanding what you have done. A simple approach that we find quite useful for understanding personality is one that was devised by Dr Eric Berne,

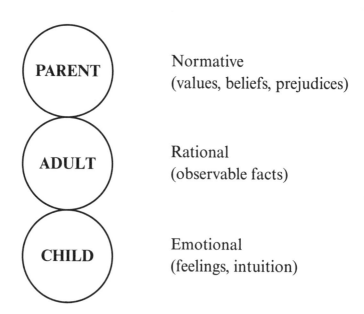

Fig 2.2 Basic ego states

author of *Games People Play*. He categorized different parts of behaviour into 'Parent', 'Adult' and 'Child' (Fig 2.2).

The meanings behind these names can sometimes be confused with the usual constructions put on these three words, but Berne takes them to refer to parts of us that deal with the world in different ways and their meaning is reflected in our thinking and in our behaviour. The Parent part of us deals with rules, prejudices, rights and wrongs, and oughts and shoulds, among other things. The parent state shows itself in two main ways:

- the Nurturing Parent
- the Critical Parent.

When we are in the nurturing state we can be developmental, caring and concerned, as a mother and father would ideally be towards their growing children. In the critical state your behaviour might be simliar to how a skilled person looks at a product and points out a defect in it. One can also be over-demanding and rebuking in the Critical Parent state, or smothering when behaving as a Nurturing Parent. Both sets of Parent behaviours have their part to play and may occur in the same person. Some people tend to vere more towards one than the other. Others tend to have these two kinds of Parent behaviours in balance, with each as likely to be demonstrated as the other. Parent behaviours reflect patterns of rules that are used to govern all or part of their lives.

The Parent in us might cause us to say that 'men don't stay at home and look after the children', or that 'shops ought not to be open on Sundays', or cause us to put our arms around a distressed person to comfort them.

The Adult is where our rational/logical thought takes place, usually in a dispassionate objective way. It can also be described as the internal manager of our personality, and in that role has three functions:

- information collecting and processing
- testing reality and probability estimating
- selecting appropriate behaviours from our repertoire in each area.

The Adult might ask 'where are we going?' and say 'the weather today is colder than yesterday'. It might also decide if it was the right time to crack a joke in a dull meeting, or to switch to the Caring Parent to support a colleague who was 'on the defensive'.

The Child state shows itself in two main ways for many people. These are:

- the Natural Child
- the Adapted Child.

The Natural Child is, not surprisingly, the part with the need for instant satisfaction. It contains all feelings, such as joy, happiness, fear, aggression, play and fantasy; it leads to creativity and taking risks, but also dependence on others.

The Adapted Child is a part of us that has learned that we cannot always do exactly what we want to do whenever we want to do it. It learns that there are rules for guidance. If it is overdeveloped, these rules limit behaviour but may lead to rebellion if we are pushed too far. It is the part that withdraws; takes our ball home, but does the right things at the right time, *when in company*. It helps us to adjust to different cultures, after our Parent has learned the local rules, or our Adult has made enquiries and established what are the local customs that we need to heed.

The Natural Child will enjoy taking part in a creativity session at work, or shouting out 'She's behind you' at a pantomime. It will also feel emotional at a wedding, and be frightened in a horror film.

The Adapted Child will behave appropriately towards the overseas visitors at work, but feel that it is difficult to argue with the boss.

We all have these different parts of our personality available to a greater or lesser degree, and it is possible to grow each of them if you judge that such development will be beneficial. Once you start to think about them, or better still, start to discuss them with someone who knows you well, you can start to see where your strong and weak areas are. They ought (parent!) to develop over time.

For most of us, as we grow older and times change, our views on what seems reasonable also change. Take, for instance, the tradition popular in some countries of playing 'trick or treat'. On Hallowe'en children dress up as witches or ghosts etc. and knock on people's doors. When the door is opened they ask the question 'trick or treat?'. If the occupant is prepared, they will reply 'treat' and will then give the children some sweets or a small present. If the occupant is unprepared or unwilling to go along with the game then the children will play a trick on them, perhaps squirting a water pistol at them or something similar.

When you are 12 or 13 this seems like fun. If you are an elderly person living alone it can seem more like a nuisance. Thus our perspectives change over time.

In order to help with the updating of our rules we have the Adult. This as we have said is the logical, dispassionate, objective side of us that functions by gathering information, unsullied by our biases, and comes to a revised view of the world, and what our rules should be. It also gathers information through the Parent and through the Child. Sometimes, if you are trained in areas such as law, engineering, or science, you may be so disciplined in being objective that the 'feelings' part of the Child is denied or suppressed. The result can be that people become out of touch with their own feelings; however, they can still be affected by them, or the lack of them.

The important part is that if you are not in touch with all three parts of yourself you may have missed chances to achieve. If you have not dared to let your hair down, not dared to let others know what you are feeling, nor chanced your arm in a risk-taking or potentially creative situation (Child), or if you have not understood the rules or etiquette in a particular work environment (Parent), or you have ignored information because your Adult is switched off, you may have missed out on opportunities to grow and develop. You may not have done things that would now be useful for further stages of your development. But it is not too late to change what you have done, and we will deal with that in the milestone called 'Where am I going?' (p. 131).

It is useful to get some idea of what you are like in terms of this way of looking at personality. You are likely to act differently in different circumstances. You may tend to depend upon one ego state more than the others, or neglect one in preference for the others. It is possible to draw circles of different sizes to represent the amount that you use each of the states.

We call these diagrams 'egograms' and a selection of these with explanations or descriptions is shown. In the Fig. 2.3 we show the way that George acts when instructing his managers about the new financial system that the company is introducing. He is telling people what to do, and his Parent is represented by a large circle. He is not using his Adult much, but he is using his free or Natural Child in order to relate to his people.

In Fig 2.4 we show the way in which George reacts when introduced to the new financial system by the systems analyst. He is asking lots of questions with his Adult, and the only Child part is the Adapted Child, who is fitting in with the way that the analyst likes to work.

In Fig 2.5 we are looking at George's behaviour in a party thrown by the Chief Executive at his house, after George's group has been

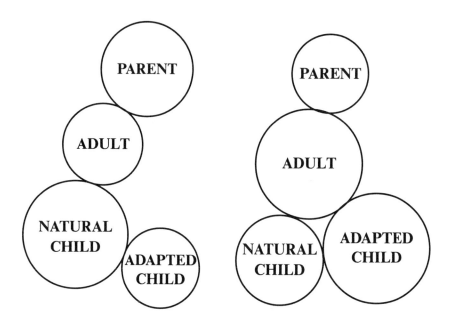

Fig 2.3 Egogram
(George giving instructions)

Fig 2.4 Egogram
(George under instruction)

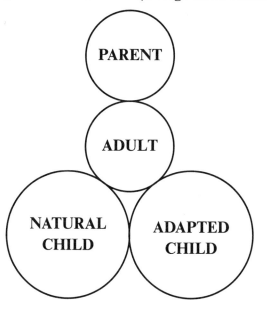

Fig 2.5 Egogram
(George at a party)

instrumental in landing a large new order with a potentially huge customer. The two Child areas are large, because George wants to enjoy himself, but does not want to be over the top. The Parent and Adult are relatively small.

Exercise 9

MY EGOGRAMS

Try some egograms for yourself. Think of a variety of past situations, and see what you are likely to be using in them.

Exercise 10

CONSOLIDATED EGOGRAM

Now think about the way you have been on average, or overall; how people have seen you in a variety of situations.

Exercise 11

MY PARENT – ADULT – CHILD DEVELOPMENT

Now think about each of the three areas (Parent, Adult, Child) in turn.

Write down developmental experiences that you have had by following or creating the rules, or where you have been in charge. Write down what experiences you have had in the areas of pure information gathering, or working logically. Finally list the experiences that have come from letting your feelings influence you, by taking risks, pushing your shyness and lack of confidence aside and letting your natural impulses out.

Parent list

_____

_____

_____

Adult list

Child list

Muse over what this tells you about your preferences in terms of these three categories. Do you need to use more of one style; less of another? Could you succeed in other areas if these changes were made, where up until now you have achieved little?

Look at these case studies; there is one for each area: Parent, Adult, Child.

Alan had attended production meetings for months. He noticed that the chairman never asked his opinion. He was not the only one who was ignored. Those who the chairman ignored were all well disciplined, and did not interrupt. People who had inter-rupted in previous meetings were now scanned by the chairman to see if they had anything to offer. Alan felt that it was rude and ignorant to butt in. His parents had taught him that, and experience in his previous job in the Civil Service had confirmed that this was the right way to behave. But he was now faced with a dilemma; to continue to be ignored, or break the habit of a lifetime. Alan interrupted (with some considerable embarrassment) at the next two meetings. After that, the chairman treated him as being present, not absent, and he did not have to go through the uncomfortable experience again.

Caroline knew that punctual attendance was highly valued in her office. People who came in late or left early were seen as lower in value than those who were in and out at the correct times. One of Caroline's contacts in the Brussels office of her company spent a lot of time in meetings and on the road, and would usually telephone Caroline only at the start of her working day, or when she broke for lunch. Caroline often found that it took days to make contact, which was most unsatisfactory. She made an appointment to see her boss, and told her about the problem. Caroline then asked whether staggering her lunch time, or starting and finishing an hour earlier than everyone else would be the best solution. It was agreed that she would start work earlier, and the boss undertook to let the CEO know Caroline's new work times, so that she suffered no 'career damage'.

Sylvia was engaged in meeting business clients to discover what more her company could do to provide customer service. She found it took her a long time to be accepted in each place that she visited; sometimes it took more than one visit. She asked Colleen, who never had to re-visit an organization, what her secret was. Colleen said that she tried to find something out about each person that she visited in the first two or three minutes, before she began discussing the areas in which she was interested. She would then enter into a discussion in which she allowed her contacts to enthuse about their interests. She would also enthuse about the subject, and usually share some humour in the interchange too. Once she was in rapport with her contacts it was easier to stay close to them, in empathy with them, as they discussed the serious questions and problems in which she was interested. Sylvia did not like the sound of this. She was paid to work, not to enjoy herself. She did not believe that she should detour away from the main area under discussion. However she tried out this approach and found that not only did it work, but her time with each customer was reduced. Both she and her contacts seemed to enjoy their interactions more than they had done previously.

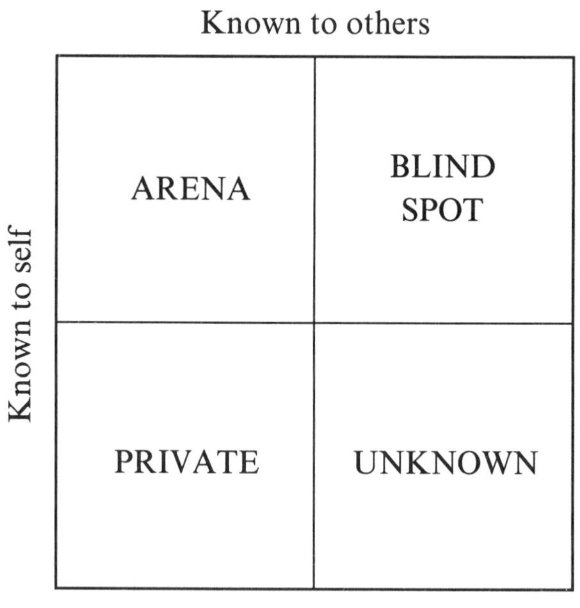

Known to others

ARENA	BLIND SPOT
PRIVATE	UNKNOWN

Known to self

Fig 2.6 Johari Window

Exercise 12

CHANGING MY PARENT, ADULT OR CHILD REACTIONS

Write down areas where a behaviour or thought change would be beneficial for you. Write down what happened and what might be done differently in the future.

_____

_____

_____

_____

_____

_____

Excuse us for dwelling on this, but, yet another way of examining our relationships with others is by looking at a model of perception that pays particular attention to how we see ourselves compared with how others see us. We used to think this was a highly sophisticated theory developed by an Eastern philosopher. However, to our surprise, we discovered it is a practical tool named after its originators – Joseph Luft and Harry Ingham – hence the name 'Johari Window'. They developed it to help them deal with feedback issues when dealing with engineers during a development programme.

Figure 2.6 represents the Johari Window as designed by Jo and Harry. This looks at how you see yourself compared with how others see you and also explores both the known and unknown areas.

First of all let us look at each of the four panes and what they represent before moving on to the practical uses of this model in exploring the question 'who am I?'.

The open window or 'arena' relates to things you and others know about yourself. For instance your name, job, age, height, eye colour and the range of other things you know about yourself and reveal to others. The more you know about yourself and reveal to others the bigger your arena. (And consequently the smaller one or all of the other panes.)

The 'blind spot' is the pane showing things other people know about you, but which you do not know about yourself. For instance such things as physical mannerisms or regular behaviour patterns in certain situations. (The individual who loses his temper with certain types of people or situations, but who sees himself as calm and controlled.) The more an individual solicits feedback from others, thus becoming aware of such things, the smaller the blind spot pane will be..

The 'private' or hidden area relates to things you know about yourself but other people do not know about you – the things you want to keep hidden. Much in this area relates to your values or perhaps some of your life experiences which you choose not to share with others. This pane can also depend on your relationship with others and the levels of closeness or trust that exist, and hence the level of self-disclosure in the relationship.

The final pane is called 'unknown' since it relates to those things hidden in our unconscious that neither yourself or others are aware of, or indeed it can be something in the future that has not yet occurred.

In terms of your own Johari Window your perception of yourself will almost certainly not be as symmetrical as the model illustrated in Fig 2.6. Typically the panes will vary in

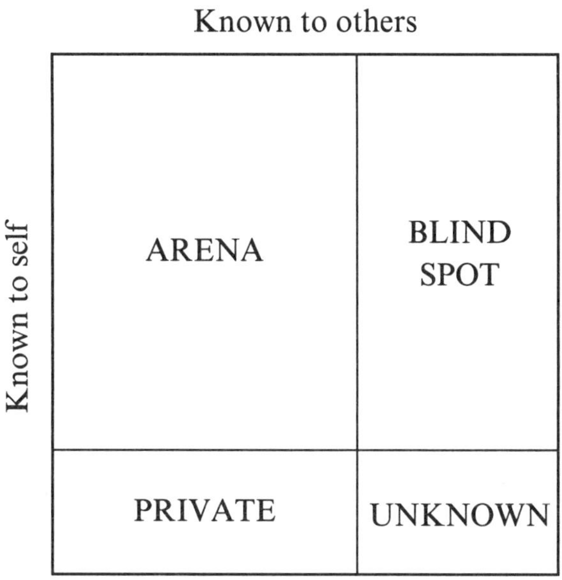

Known to others

Known to self

| ARENA | BLIND SPOT |
| PRIVATE | UNKNOWN |

Fig 2.7 Johari Window (with a loved one)

size and indeed they may possibly vary quite a lot in different relationships and situations.

For instance, with a loved one it might look something like Fig 2.7:

This has a very large arena illustrating the closeness, trust and sharing that exists in the relationship.

With an individual or a group you have just met it might look like Fig 2.8. This has a small arena and blind spot, but a large private area and unknown area, due to the newness of the relationship and the lack of trust as yet.

In terms of analysing 'who am I'? you may find it a useful device to attempt to draw your own Johari Window for some of the relationships you find yourself in.

Known to others

ARENA	BLIND SPOT
PRIVATE	UNKNOWN

Known to self

Fig 2.8 Johari Window (with a new group)

Exercise 13

MY JOHARI WINDOWS

Think of some of the key relationships in your life and draw a Johari Window for each one.

Now ask yourself:

● What does this tell me about myself in this relationship?
● Am I happy with it?
● How does this make me feel?
● Could I make some adjustments to make the relationship more effective?

The visible portion of you, which we refer to as your behaviours, is all the things you say and do. These behaviours are so apparent to everyone with whom you come into contact that inevitably they have a direct effect on other people. Of course your behaviours will vary according to the situations in which you find yourself. As far as others are concerned you are to a large degree your behaviour, because they cannot observe your underlying thoughts, motives, attitudes or feelings. Clearly, your behaviour influences the following two areas:

- *Other people's perceptions of you*
  i.e. whether they like or dislike you, trust or mistrust you, respect and admire you
- *Other people's reactions to you*
  i.e. whether they behave helpfully or unhelpfully, co-operatively or competitively towards you.

This whole area of relationships is complex and is influenced by your thoughts, motives, attitudes and feelings, these are usually very private and are much less likely to surface directly in their raw state for others to witness. When they are demonstrated to the outside world they are often very good indicators of your values. We will return to your values later in this milestone.

FOCUS ON YOUR BEHAVIOURS/SKILLS

At this stage let us concentrate on the behaviours that you exhibit to the outside world – that portion of the iceberg above the surface of the water, or your 'arena'. We all have a repertoire of behaviours which when demonstrated and practised often enough become effective skills. As with the acquisition of any skill it requires a conscious effort because each skill is practised to the point where it becomes effortless. A good example of a skill in the context of work is the ability to conduct effective interviews. Interviewing is a skill based upon thorough preparation and a series of behavioural techniques such as non-verbal communication, questioning, etc. To do it successfully requires you to adapt your behaviours to suit particular interviewing situations. It is possible to learn the correct behaviours and improve your skill without affecting or impinging on any of those deeper aspects of yourself which are usually more difficult to change. But as with all forms of self-improvement, you have to start by having a good understanding of what your present repertoire of skills comprises.

Yours is not the only view of course. Asking yourself the question 'who am I?' in terms of your skills involves exploring your repertoire from a variety of different perspectives. The three major outlets for gaining this type of awareness are:

- *Self-perceptions*
  Your structured thoughts and feelings about your own skills
- *Others' perceptions*
  Feedback from others (friends, relatives, colleagues or anyone with whom you have a learning relationship) on what they see as being your full range of skills
- *Formal frameworks*
  Information taken from appraisals, career counselling and all forms of assessment, including psychometric tests and inventories.

Let us begin by looking at your own view of your strengths and weaknesses. Stop and think for a while because they may not be as obvious to you as you might expect. Take the case of Chris Jones for example.

Chris left school at 16 and after serving a four-year apprenticeship became a Quality Control Inspector on the shop floor of a large

Aeroengine factory. He was very competent at his job, which required good mathematical skills, attention to detail and a good mechanical aptitude. Quite surprisingly one of the things which he enjoyed most was talking with, and establishing, a warm, trusting relationship with many of the men whose engineering components he was meant to be checking.

Eventually the desire to relate with others and listen to their problems became so overwhelming that Chris began to reassess how his skills might help him to further his career. He took redundancy and went off to study psychology as a mature student at university. He now works as a professional psychologist and cites as less-used the three skills that he used so successfully on the shop floor as a mechanical engineer – mathematical skills, attention to detail and mechanical aptitude.

Now reflect on what you think your major strengths and weaknesses are. Before you write down your strengths be aware that there are a couple of common traps that people tend to fall into when attempting this sort of exercise. Concentrate on what you really think you are good at – not on what you would like to think you are good at. And finally, ask yourself 'is it really a strength or is it something that I just seem to do very often?'.

Exercise 14

MY STRENGTHS AND WEAKNESSES REVIEW

My strengths – my view

_____

_____

_____

Now write down your weaknesses, and remember, since nobody else has to see this document, ask yourself *is it a totally honest assessment*? Also, try and distinguish between what you think is a general weakness and one which might be much more situational.

My weaknesses – my view

_____

_____

_____

_____

_____

_____

The next part of this exercise is a bit more difficult than you might initially think. Try to put yourself in the shoes of others (sounds easy, but it is not) and ask yourself 'what would they cite as being my major strengths and weaknesses?'. If it is hard to assume the perspective of work colleagues, think about what your friends and your family might say. They might not say it directly to you, but people often allude to what they think are your strengths and weaknesses through casual or informal conversation. In terms of both your strengths and your weaknesses ask yourself 'are there any common themes that a number of others would highlight?'. Also ask 'what situations do different people (identify them perhaps) see me in? Is this significant?'.

My strengths – others' views

_____

_____

_____

_____

_____

_____

My weaknesses – others' views

_____

_____

_____

_____

_____

Finally consider what formal frameworks such as appraisals, psychometric tests/inventories, or any form of career counselling session, appear to be suggesting about your skills. Again try to draw out any common themes that emerge from the data and put it into the sort of language that you are best able to understand. For example, a statement such as 'John is very effective in dealing with customers' might mean either that he listens well or is very polite with them, or indeed, a variety of other things.

My strengths – formal frameworks

_____

_____

_____

_____

_____

_____

My weaknesses – formal frameworks

_____

_____

_____

_____

_____

_____

Before you leave this concentration on your strengths and weaknesses think back to the case of Chris and how his skills changed over a period of time. Now think about your own strengths. In terms of their value which of your strengths have been the most valuable to you in the past? It is also important to note those that have endured over a lengthy period of time.

Exercise 15

MY STRENGTHS AND WEAKNESSES ANALYSIS

My most valuable past strengths *My enduring past strengths*

_____ _____

_____ _____

_____ _____

_____ _____

_____ _____

Now consider your present strengths across your whole life by asking yourself 'why are these of value now?'.

My present strengths

_____

_____

_____

_____

_____

_____

Finally, think about the future and speculate on which of these strengths are likely to endure.

My future strengths

_____

_____

_____

_____

_____

_____

_____

Now do the same with your weaknesses noting down those that have been the most restrictive to you in the past. It is also most important to try and recognize those that have been difficult to change over a lengthy period of time, and try to understand why.

My past weaknesses

_____

_____

_____

_____

_____

_____

_____

Now consider your present weaknesses across your whole life by asking yourself 'why do I perceive these as weaknesses now?'.

My recent weaknesses

_____

_____

_____

_____

_____

_____

_____

Finally, think about the future and ask yourself 'which do I really want or need to do something about?'

My development areas

_____

_____

_____

_____

_____

_____

_____

FOCUS ON YOUR VALUES

Using the analogy of an iceberg we suggested to you earlier that the greatest part of who you are (90%) sits below the surface of the water where no-one else can see it easily. We then went on to assert that those parts of you that are most hidden from the outside world are often rooted in your values. Although we are not aware of it all the time, we all give our lives direction through what might be called a private 'philosophy of life'. This is founded upon a set of personal values or basic convictions about what is, and what is not, of real importance in life. They are central to the way you would like to live. With respect to the journey you are on – they are your *key drivers*.

Research by psychologists indicates that people's core or deepest values revolve around the following six aspects: the theoretical, economic, artistic, social, political and spiritual.

The theoretical

This is the degree to which a person, group, or society, is concerned with the discovery of truth, assuming a cerebral or thinking attitude in pursuing this objective. This stems from interests that are rational, critical, and ultimately based upon observation and practical experience. The sort of person who holds this value is one who is very questioning, likes discussion, and continually wants to get to the bottom of things. When on a training programme, or in any group lecture situation, the theoretical person enjoys quizzing the tutor on a lot of his/her assertions and assumptions.

The economic

This is the degree to which a person, group or society, is interested in practicality and usefulness for the sake of economic self-preservation. To a large degree this is motivated by success in the world of work, resulting in the accumulation of wealth and material goods. In their relations with others economic persons tend to be more interested in comparing and surpassing them in wealth, rather than satisfying any underlying social needs. A good example of the emphasis on practicality and usefulness is their attitude to education and learning. For economic persons its only value is when it is practical and useful. Unapplied knowledge is regarded as waste. Ultimately economic persons get things done.

The artistic

This is the degree to which a person, group or society is interested in and motivated by form and harmony in all things (not only the creative arts). In other words, their chief interest is in the artistic or creative episodes of life. The sort of person who holds this value is one who looks at objects, people and language, and whose first inclination is to reflect on the feelings of aesthetic beauty it creates. For artistic people the sense of wonderment never diminishes when looking at objectively beautiful events such as sunsets. These people are also capable of finding beauty in even the most simple, mundane things in life.

The social

This is the degree to which a person, group, or society, is interested in and motivated towards drawing people together. Such people prize others for their human qualities and are themselves kind, sympathetic and unselfish. For the social person life is all about people and the everyday realities of social life. Nothing gives them greater pleasure than being in and with groups of people who are working in harmony with each other.

The political

This is the degree to which a person, group, or society is interested in and motivated by the struggle for influence and power.

Such people take the view that struggle is 'the stuff of life' and therefore yearn for personal power, influence and renown. The sort of person who holds this value is one who strives to be the leader when involved in any form of leaderless group discussion or activity. For such people usually the issue, whether it be political, work or family related, comes second to the fact that they have to influence others and be seen to be in charge.

The spiritual

This is the degree to which a person, group, or society, struggles with understanding and experiencing the world as a united whole, consisting of some sort of higher meaning. Such people are oriented towards a search for the highest and most satisfying value experience – a sense of growth and inner calm. For such persons this value orientation manifests itself in very different ways. For example, some may tend towards a spirituality that expresses itself within the context of everyday life and may involve caring for others or going to a religious institution regularly. Others may strive towards a spirituality that encourages them to live apart from everyday life, for example, hermits or monks. Regardless of the particular type of expression, the spiritual person is one who believes in something that transcends the physical world; a faith that ultimately gives them inner calm and contentment.

Most of your values will be contained within these six themes. In order to bring them to life and make them clearer you may like to imagine the following scenario:

Six individuals each representing one of the core value orientations are walking together through the woods on a sunny autumn afternoon. The theoretical individual is thinking about the growth and development of the trees and how the wood came about. The economic individual wonders about the viability of chopping down some of the trees and converting them to toothpicks to make some money. The artistic individual is happy to frolic in the leaves and take in the beauty of the surroundings. The social individual gains contentment just from being in the company of five other friendly people. The political individual finds it difficult to refrain from leading the group through a particular path, insisting that it is the correct way. And finally, the spiritual person gets lost in thoughts concerning the ultimate reality of what these people and woods represent.

The theoretical, economic, artistic, social, political and spiritual, are what we refer to as your 'core values'. Obviously no single individual holds only one of these values; we are all a complex mix. In many ways they reflect who you are and why you do what you do. At a more specific level, various issues relating to these themes underpin many of what we refer to as your 'external values' – those closer to the surface and more recognizable to others.

Exercise 16

MY VALUES REVIEW

The exercise has been designed to assist you in reviewing both your core and external values. Think about the importance of each value in terms of situations that occur across the major areas of your life, particularly at work. Rate the importance of each as follows:

Always   A value you have in your life every day
Often   A strong value, but not as important as always
Sometimes   Important, but you would be willing to compromise
Rarely   Not very important
Never   Holds no value for you

	Always	*Often*	*Sometimes*	*Rarely*	*Never*

THEORETICAL

Critical inquiry

Continually asking complex
questions and participating in
demanding tasks, trouble-
shooting and problem-solving
as a core part of a job.

	☐	☐	☐	☐	☐

Focus on the new

Work in research and
development, generating
information and new ideas in
the business, academic or
scientific communities.

	☐	☐	☐	☐	☐

Intellectual curiosity

Engage in the pursuit of
knowledge, truth and
understanding.

	☐	☐	☐	☐	☐

Intellectual status

Be regarded as very well
informed and a strong
theorist; as a specialist in a
given field.

	☐	☐	☐	☐	☐

	Always	*Often*	*Sometimes*	*Rarely*	*Never*

ECONOMIC

Achievement
Be able to get ahead rapidly, gaining opportunities for growth and seniority from work well done.

☐ ☐ ☐ ☐ ☐

Competition
Engage in activities which pit my abilities against others.

☐ ☐ ☐ ☐ ☐

Profit
Have strong likelihood of accumulating large amounts of money or other useful/practical gains through ownership, profit-sharing, commissions, merit pay increases and the like.

☐ ☐ ☐ ☐ ☐

Security
Concentrate on the practicalities of keeping my job and a reasonable financial reward.

☐ ☐ ☐ ☐ ☐

	Always	*Often*	*Sometimes*	*Rarely*	*Never*

ARTISTIC

Aesthetic appreciation
Be involved in studying or
appreciating the beauty of
things or ideas.

☐ ☐ ☐ ☐ ☐

Artistic creativity
Use a sense of form and
harmony by engaging in
creative work in any of
several art forms.

☐ ☐ ☐ ☐ ☐

Creative expression
Be able to express in writing
and in person my ideas
concerning my job and how
I might improve it; have
opportunities for
experimentation and
innovation.

☐ ☐ ☐ ☐ ☐

General creativity
Create new ideas, plans,
innovative structures or
anything that does not follow
a format developed by others.

☐ ☐ ☐ ☐ ☐

	Always	*Often*	*Sometimes*	*Rarely*	*Never*

SOCIAL

Affiliation
Be recognized as a member of a particular organization.

☐	☐	☐	☐	☐

Altruism
Be involved in helping people directly, either individually or in small groups, believing that this contributes to the betterment of the world.

☐	☐	☐	☐	☐

Friendships
Develop close personal relationships with people as a result of work activity.

☐	☐	☐	☐	☐

Social interaction
Having a lot of day-to-day contact with people.

☐	☐	☐	☐	☐

	Always	*Often*	*Sometimes*	*Rarely*	*Never*

POLITICAL

Influence others
Put myself in a position to change attitudes or opinions of other people.

| | ☐ | ☐ | ☐ | ☐ | ☐ |

Decision-making
Have the power to decide courses of action and/or policies and use judgements that affect the lives of others.

| | ☐ | ☐ | ☐ | ☐ | ☐ |

Power and authority
Control the work activities or destinies of others.

| | ☐ | ☐ | ☐ | ☐ | ☐ |

Status
Impress or gain the respect of others by using the nature and/or level of responsibility of my work to achieve things.

| | ☐ | ☐ | ☐ | ☐ | ☐ |

	Always	*Often*	*Sometimes*	*Rarely*	*Never*

SPIRITUAL

Inner tranquillity
Have ways of avoiding
pressures and the 'rat race'
in all life-roles.

☐	☐	☐	☐	☐

Moral fulfilment
Feel that my work is
contributing to ideals I
consider very important.

☐	☐	☐	☐	☐

Spiritual growth
Be continually on the
look-out for situations that
give me opportunities
to enhance my spiritual
development.

☐	☐	☐	☐	☐

Whole person
Be content that each of my
life-roles are complementary
parts of what I consider to be
a unified whole.

☐	☐	☐	☐	☐

Before going on to summarize your own values, consider the following brief case study:

A friend of ours called Nicola discovered that, after completing the Values Review, most of her prominent values were in either the theoretical or the social areas. Prior to having two children she had worked as a senior secretary in a major electronics firm. As her children were growing up she was desperately keen to return to a job that gave her more personal satisfaction than her previous occupation. She always knew that she was interested in the caring professions and was quite attracted by the idea of becoming a social worker. Unfortunately Nicola was put off by the thought of gaining the academic qualifications that she would need in order to be a social worker, because she did not think that she was capable of studying to the level required. To our delight Nicola was so impressed by the fact that the Values Review highlighted her theoretical inclinations, she had the confidence to start believing in herself. She is currently in her final year of study to become a qualified social worker. Apparently she has particularly impressed her tutors and peers with her ability to analyse and debate complex human welfare issues.

Exercise 17

WHAT ARE MY VALUES?

Now review the items you ticked as always important and select the six that are most prominent in your life. List them below.

Value review table

My obvious values are:	Note down the core value categories each value comes from e.g. theoretical, economic, etc.
1.	
2.	
3.	
4.	
5.	
6.	

How does this make you think or feel?

_____

_____

Distinguish between those values that are currently being met in your life and those that are not. This can be difficult, but by becoming clearer about your values you can achieve a better understanding of why you are interested in the things that you are interested in (at home and at work). If your values are not being lived out through your interests, or if your interests do not reflect your values, it can lead to unhappiness. Filling in your happiness review and relating it back to your values should provide you with an even greater understanding of the nature of your values and how they are being lived out.

Exercise 18

MY HAPPINESS REVIEW

Write down in order of preference the things that have made you happy over the last 12 months, both at work and at home.

Work   *Home*

_____   _____

_____   _____

_____   _____

_____   _____

_____   _____

Now write down in order of preference the things that have made you unhappy over the last 12 months, both at work and at home.

Work   *Home*

_____   _____

_____   _____

_____   _____

_____   _____

_____   _____

If you are still not entirely clear whether you are living out your values to your own satisfaction, which at the end of the day is the only thing that matters, try to complete this final exercise. In our experience people usually find it useful to compare the real, down-to-earth view of their life so far, with a more ideal view. Put another way, if you were asked by your partner or one of your family to describe your life to date you would probably tell it as it is. Now if asked to do the same thing to somebody who you were very keen to impress (for example a prospective employer at a job selection interview) the story would probably sound a little different. People always have a 'real' and 'ideal' view of themselves and their life; so be honest and fill in your obituary.

Exercise 19

MY OBITUARY

Imagine having to write your own obituary. Prepare two versions of it to appear in *The Times* newspaper.
One which reflects your life to date:

_____

_____

_____

_____

_____

_____

One which you would ideally like to see:

_____

_____

_____

_____

_____

_____

_____

_____

Is there a mismatch and if so what does it tell you about your personal values?

_____

_____

_____

_____

_____

_____

_____

_____

SUMMARY

In this milestone we have encouraged you to delve deep into who you are; the key areas explored are:

- Ways of examining your self-perceptions
- How you can review your perceptions of how others see you
- Your values and how these affect who you are
- Your strengths and weaknesses viewed from a variety of perspectives.

Well done! The effort that you have invested in working through this section should have given you a much clearer understanding of who you are. Use it as the springboard for the rest of your journey, but do not be afraid to return to it if you get diverted at any point along the way.

MILESTONE 2

What have I done?

'...never let your chances like the millstream pass you by...'
BEATRICE MAY HAGGER

Here we want you to explore what you have done in your life. We examine what you have done in a variety of different ways. We encourage you to explore what you have done in your life from the perspective of 'achievements'. By looking at life experiences as achievements we hope that you can begin to understand the wide variety of opportunities available to you in managing your own development.

So we have encouraged you to look at who you are. Now it is time to look at what you have done, perhaps because of, or indeed in spite of, who you are. It could be argued that you are what you have done, as much as you are anything else. It could also be argued that you are shaped by what you have not done, and even by what you would have wanted to do, or feel that you ought to have done. It may be that this is the time to catch up on some unfinished business that you feel events or people prevented you from doing in the past. You might also be one of those 'preventers' from the past, for yourself or for others. You could be an obstacle to your own progress, and it may be time to give yourself permission to go where you have not permitted yourself previously to travel. 'To go where no man (or woman) has gone before!' as it says in the log of the Starship Enterprise.

This milestone concentrates on what we have done with our lives so far, and sometimes hints at what we could do from now on. The future is dealt with in more detail in the milestone 'Where am I going?' (p.131).

Here we want you to be concerned with the many areas of your achievements. These could encompass both tangible and intangible things. Tangible things are often quite easy to reflect on and get some measure of their importance. Intangible achievements can be measured, but not with the same precision because they are usually not very concrete. In thinking about what you have done we ask you not to be modest or shy, and not to deny that an achievement exists. If it feels like an achievement, whether or not you have ever mentioned your feelings about it to anyone else, it is an achievement!

What you have done can also be viewed from a timescale perspective, and may have been achieved by you either as an individual or as part of a group or team. We will be encouraging you to view your achievements in all these ways in later exercises.

Other variables that we believe you will find it useful to explore are competences that you have (see Exercise 26: Competence review p.101), roles that you have played in and out of work, different types of achievement, and recognition (or lack of it) by others and by yourself. Some of the exercises will help you summarize and recall your achievements, and make you aware of just how much you have done in your life. Most important of all, this section may remind you of events and steps that can be brought to the surface, revised, and used in new contexts in order to further your progress along the way from one milestone to another.

So let's look at these variable ways of viewing what you have done – your achievements. Firstly have a look at different timescales and what they might imply.

TIMESCALES AND ACHIEVEMENTS

Let's start by considering timescales. The Chinese have a saying that even a journey of a thousand miles starts with a single step. A good starting point here would be to draw your own lifeline, so here are a couple of examples drawn in different ways (Fig 3.1

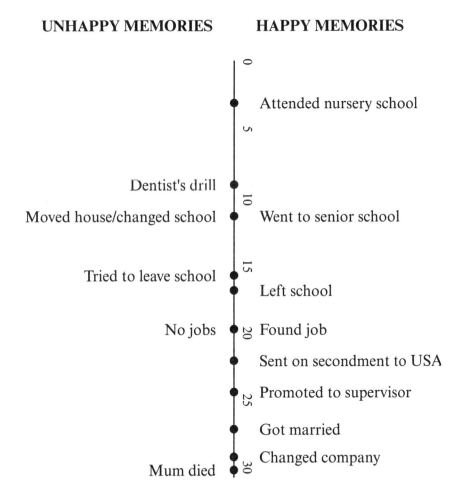

UNHAPPY MEMORIES   HAPPY MEMORIES

- Attended nursery school
- Dentist's drill
- Moved house/changed school — Went to senior school
- Tried to leave school
- Left school
- No jobs — Found job
- Sent on secondment to USA
- Promoted to supervisor
- Got married
- Changed company
- Mum died

Fig 3.1

and 3.2). It is important that you draw your lifeline in a way that has meaning for you.

Typically the lifeline is started by having time intervals set out along it. These could be in five-year spans as illustrated, or you could vary the intervals for different times of your life, perhaps by moving to one-year intervals when there was a lot going on. It might be that you need to move to months for certain times when a lot happened at once; but earlier or later stages in your life might not have been as congested, and you could revert to a scale measured in years once more.

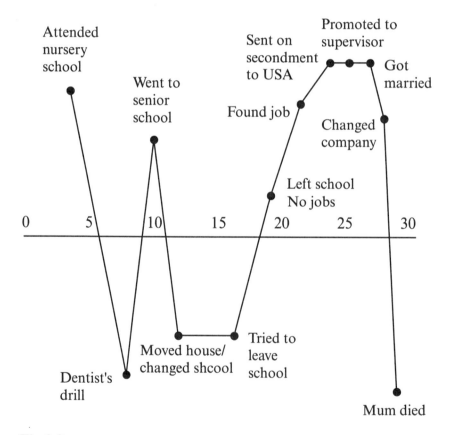

Fig 3.2

The lifeline is annotated with key events in your life as they occur to you. People usually find it easy to start at the beginning, but some find it more useful to move around as memories are recalled. In the first diagram important points are placed along a straight line; in the second they rise and fall in relation to some factor that is important in your eyes.

Now try drawing a lifeline for yourself.

Exercise 20

MY LIFELINE

Take a sheet of A4, or even A3 paper if you have one available, and draw your own lifeline, annotating it in order to make it meaningful.

Then ask yourself how you felt about each experience. Was it a high point or low point in your life? Are there things that differentiate between my high and low points? What have I learned from:

● my high points?
● my low points?

(You may wish to note these learning points for later use in the milestone 'How did I Learn?' p.111)

What did you achieve when you went through this experience? You may want to rate these recalled experiences in other ways. For instance:

● Was it a long or short experience?
● If there was an achievement, did I do it alone, or with the help of others?
● Did it expand my horizons?
● Was I taken into and did I manage to cope with a different culture?
● Was this an important experience for me?

Once you have drawn the basic lifeline, you may want to go into different types of detail with it. You might ask yourself the above or other questions, or look for some kind of patterns that you want to retain or replace in the future.

If you are still not clear about your achievements go back to your strengths in 'Who Am I?' (p.30) and think about how you developed those strengths.

Another aspect of timescales worthy of consideration is the length of time that it took you to do something. Does this change the value of that activity in your eyes or the eyes of others? If you found it easy to pass your specialist exams, and you took the minimum time to do so, is that better or worse than if you had slogged away grimly for years to get to the same point on the map?

Sometimes we may feel that things we do quickly are easy, and could be done easily by anyone, therefore they are not as valuable to others or to us as the things that we find difficult – those things that cause sweat, tears and tiredness, if not actually making us draw blood in the process! And yet that speed of achievement might reflect an intangible success, such as quickly seeing connections between ideas that for others are not connected. It could be a sign of creativity. Take this example:

In a computer training session, Wilf was listening to the trainer telling the class how to 'click' on to an icon or symbol on the computer screen, using the device called 'a mouse', and then to 'drag' the icon into a more convenient space. He heard the trainer tell the group to use the mouse to 'drag' and then 'drop' the symbol elsewhere. Without thinking, he said 'I suppose you call those mouse droppings ?'. He then thought to himself 'I expect the trainer has

*heard that a million times before, and I've been boringly obvious',
but when he asked, she said it was new to her.*

So things that come easily to you, particularly at work, may be
insights that lead to achievements, or indeed achievements in
their own right, even though they may not be as obvious to others as you assume. Particularly in Britain, there is a tendency to
believe that if we in the UK think of an idea, then the value of
that idea must be smaller than if it comes from Japan, Germany,
the USA and so on.

Sometimes we feel that there is more credit due to those who
have taken a long time over doing something, and perhaps by
implication overcome more difficulties than the rapid achiever.
It is almost like thinking that medicine has to have a disgusting
taste before it can improve your condition.

You can now put your own perspectives on to timescales.

*Helen took a job that she considered would not extend her, in order
to have the chance to aim for the next job in the organization. She
gave herself 18 months to secure the next job. In the event, she was
promoted in 15 months, when the manager whom she replaced was
herself promoted. Helen had analysed her manager's job, and
worked out what she needed to achieve in order to become a con-
tender for the job when the position became vacant. She got herself onto training courses, and volunteered to work at unpopular
shift times in order to demonstrate her capacity for responsibility,
and to learn about things that until then she had not had to deal
with. When the company looked around for a natural successor to
her boss, she stood out from the crowd.*

You could say that each new skill she acquired was an incre-
mental achievement in itself, but we are focusing on the longer
timescale, and her promotion. You could consider both the

overall success, and the steps along the way, as separate achievements.

So the next exercise may help you reflect on the different times that your achievements took to happen. You may find it difficult to do at this moment, but give it a try. If you are not too successful now, wait until later in this section, when you are more 'warmed up' to the concept of achievement, and try this exercise again.

Think of Cecil Rhodes, who discovered, and developed or exploited (subjectively different views exist of what is and what is not an achievement too) the country that used to be known as Rhodesia. It is reputed that on his gravestone is written 'So little done, so much to do', and yet his achievements could seem huge and they certainly covered a large time-span from the perspective of the 'average man or woman in the street'.

Exercise 21

MY ACHIEVEMENT TIMESCALES

Think of something that you have achieved, like a professional qualification, or reaching a particular position in your company. Write it down, and next to it, put how long it took from starting or even thinking about it for the first time, until it was accepted by you and others that you had done whatever you were considering.

Achievement   *Timescale*

_____   _____

_____   _____

_____   _____

Now think of some of your other achievements – both tangible and intangible – and write them down with the timescale alongside. You may find that you prefer to state the timescale in years or months; or maybe, particularly for the intangibles, use less specific terms. You could have a scale from 'instant' through 'short', 'medium' and 'long' to 'lifetime'.

_____

_____

_____

_____

_____

_____

Now return to the list, ponder, and ask yourself the following questions:

● Are you glad that you have done these things?
● Could you now see a way to have done them faster, or better, or just differently?
● Would you want to change how you operated if you were able to re-visit these areas in some kind of time-machine?
● Can these achievements be accelerated or different ways be used to achieve a present ambition? (We deal with 'Where am I going?' in the next-but-one milestone see p.131.)
● Can you push back the boundary lines that have so far limited your achievements?

Another interesting question to ask yourself is – can we learn how to achieve by looking at examples from the lives of famous people, who at school were underachievers? It is perhaps strange how often they did not start off as if they would get very far, or achieve very much.

Winston Churchill achieved fame both as the British Prime Minister who played a big part in winning the Second World War, and before that as a well-known newspaper correspondent, who was always in the thick of the action, in the Boer War. He also won the Nobel Prize for literature in 1953. But at school he was around the bottom of the class, not the top.

Hitler started off as a house-painter and was a corporal in the First World War, but he became one of the most powerful and influential men in the world.

Like Churchill, David Attenborough had poor school reports; so poor that he hid them from his academically achieving father. Then he discovered that his hobby of looking at flowers, bugs, insects and animals was also a legitimate area of scientific study, and later he was able through the medium of television both to entertain and educate thousands, if not millions, of people.

One of the Manchester United footballers who died in the Munich air crash in 1958 was said by a colleague, who did National Service with him in the army, to be as thick as two short planks off the football field, but to be an instinctive football genius on it.

Derek was a househusband staying at home with his son while his wife was out at work in her full-time job. One day, after looking at some articles in a magazine, he decided that he could write his own story in an interesting way. He did so, was paid for the article, and has now started sending articles about other aspects of his family experience to various magazines and is having those published too.

Monique was the tea-lady at a restaurant in a local firm. She had married quite young, and not continued her education as she would have liked. When people came along to her restaurant she learned all their different likes and dislikes regarding their tea and coffee preferences, and gradually got to know them more deeply. She recognized when they were feeling down, and began to comfort them. She enrolled on a counselling course, and is now some way towards a professional qualification.

So you do not have to be good at everything; nor can you expect to be. But you can make the best use of what you have done – that is, if you can handle yourself, and appreciate yourself. Some people find it hard to accept compliments. They deny their successes when people first try to praise them, or they become embarrassed. So their behaviour tends to stop people trying to pay them compliments, and then they feel that they are not appreciated for what they are doing or have done. They undervalue their achievements, or think that others do.

If you understand yourself, perhaps in terms of relatively simple ways of describing the whole person, then you can fit your knowledge of yourself into some kind of framework, and give that knowledge more coherence, a more useful meaning. At this stage it might be useful to refer back to frameworks like 'Johari Window' or the 'Parent – Adult – Child' (p.40) model referred to in 'Who Am I?' (p.37). Clearly your personality often affects how you see yourself and can be useful in understanding what you have done.

Another aspect of timescales that is worthy of consideration and of direct relevance to self-managed development is the

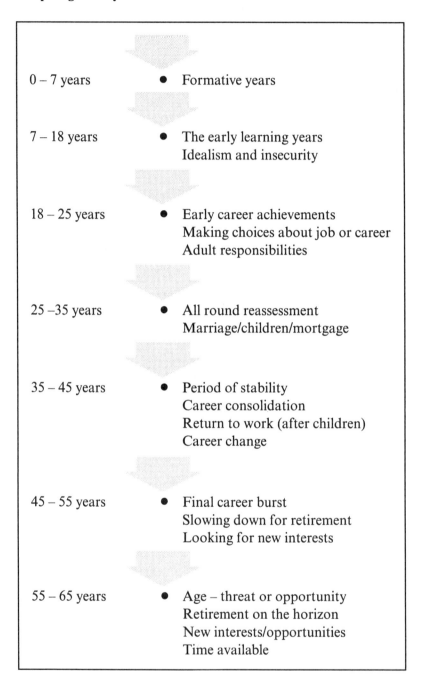

0 – 7 years	● Formative years
7 – 18 years	● The early learning years Idealism and insecurity
18 – 25 years	● Early career achievements Making choices about job or career Adult responsibilities
25 –35 years	● All round reassessment Marriage/children/mortgage
35 – 45 years	● Period of stability Career consolidation Return to work (after children) Career change
45 – 55 years	● Final career burst Slowing down for retirement Looking for new interests
55 – 65 years	● Age – threat or opportunity Retirement on the horizon New interests/opportunities Time available

Fig 3.3 Career/life stages

whole idea of a life or career stage. Many of us will be affected by the wide variety of life and career stages through which we pass. The availability of time (and money), our motivations, our needs and demands may well change and are very often affected by the particular life or career phase we are going through.

Consider Fig 3.3 which illustrates a series of typical life stages that many of us experience. You might like to reflect on your own life stage – perhaps using your own definitions.

Exercise 22

MY LIFE STAGE

Describe your current life stage.

_____

_____

_____

_____

_____

How does this affect your current achievement levels? Think about both the positive and negative.

_____

_____

_____

_____

_____

What do you feel about this?

_____

_____

_____

_____

_____

Apart from looking at timescales you can also examine your achievements from a wide variety of different perspectives for instance:

- work
- education
- hobbies
- relationships
- sports.

Perhaps you can think of your own categories in attempting the next exercise.

Exercise 23

CLASSIFYING MY ACHIEVEMENTS

Write down your achievements by area and see if there could be any transfer from one area to another. (A similar exercise is no. 32: 'My learning review'.)

_____

_____

_____

Earlier in this book, in the section entitled 'What is self-managed development?' (p.8), we explored and explained the whole concept of 'learning relationships'. This is yet another way of looking at your achievements. While you may see others as your role model, mentor or coach, what about you? What roles have you held in life, or indeed do you currently hold – both formal and informal?

Exercise 24:

MY LIFE ROLES

Think about the roles you have held throughout your life so far; what have they meant for you and what achievements can you link to these roles? List them below.

Role	*Relationship with*	*Achievements/ Meaning for me*

THE BENEFITS OF SYNERGY

Another way to view achievements is to look at combinations of the things that you have achieved, and by this method, selecting from different areas, see a possibility for a synergy from within yourself. Putting these factors from different experience areas together may give you a whole that is bigger than the sum of the parts. You could call this 'internal synergy'.

Richard was thinking back one evening to a situation at work where he was not sure what to do. He was suddenly asked to address a large group of visiting technologists who had been on a tour of the works, and was taken by surprise. He got flustered, and did not do himself justice .

At home he was wondering how he could have handled it better, and recalled the time at his previous company when he had the responsibility for giving a talk to a group of apprentices. He arranged for refreshments to be served to them just before he started, and encouraged them to eat and drink as he spoke. They appreciated his actions, and gave him a fair hearing. He had also, in his role as a member of the school parents' committee, been partly responsible for running a race night. Just before the first race, he encouraged the guests to take a comfort break, as this gave him their undivided attention when he described the procedure for the first time.

He realized that if he was ever caught out like this again, he could combine elements of both experiences. He could encourage the visitors to take a comfort break, and quickly organize tea and biscuits, so that they would be both refreshed, and aware that he was conscious of their needs. While they were involved in these two activities, he would have had time to nip to his office to collect one or two facts and some overhead projector slides to make his off-the-cuff presentation seem more professional.

Exercise 25

FINDING INTERNAL SYNERGY

Think about something you have done recently, that could have gone better. Think of other areas of your life from which two or more successes could have been transferred and combined to produce a satisfactory outcome.

_____

_____

_____

_____

_____

_____

COMPETENCES EXPLORED

Another way to look at your achievements is to examine them from a competence perspective. Our definition of competence is 'specific knowledge or skill displayed and put into practice appropriately'. Competence is very much a current management buzz-word but its use does seem to be more than a passing phase. We mentioned earlier that many organizations now measure competences as an integral part of their performance review system. Not only do many of us now have sets of competences against which we will be reviewed and rewarded in our jobs but many development programmes are also built around them. With this in mind we have developed the following list which is useful in a self-managed development context.

Competence list

Individual skills

- Controlling and managing yourself
  Organizing yourself and channelling your energy towards productive ends; keeping calm in stressful situations.

- Logical and critical thinking
  Structuring your thoughts into rational frameworks, then using these for critical evaluation and analysing your own and others' ideas.

- Managing time
  Allocating priorities, thinking through and making productive use of time available.

- Managing uncertainty and ambiguity
  Being prepared to move away from familiar ways of thinking and working, and dealing with uncertain situations comfortably.

- Creativity
  Having a sense of originality and being able to input new ideas. Arriving at new solutions to old problems.

- Self-confidence and assertiveness
  Demonstrating a belief in yourself, and being able to express what you feel is right in social and work situations. Ultimately being able to say no when others want you to say yes.

- Communication – spoken and written
  Expressing yourself clearly when talking to people, speaking at meetings, making formal and fluent presentations and writing effectively.

- Listening

   Being attentive to people's views and ideas. Giving time and being patient in order to understand their concerns, feelings and interpretations on issues.

- Problem-solving and decision-making

   Being able to think through and work with the diverse elements of a problem, then integrating the elements and making a decision.

- Self-development and learning

   Taking responsibility and control for your own development and learning. Planning your future direction.

Managing relationships

- Performance management

   Agreeing, monitoring and achieving performance standards and targets in key result areas.

- Networking

   Identifying and building a cluster of mutually beneficial relationships and developing a wide range of contacts.

- Delegating

   Developing others by passing on some of your authority and responsibility for tasks in a systematic way, thus giving you time to take on more challenging tasks from your boss.

- Influencing

   Adapting behaviour and communication style to influence and gain commitment from people in a wide range of areas and at all levels.

- Handling others' difficulties

  Helping others by acting as a counsellor, mentor and coach in order to assist in working through their personal difficulties.

- Interviewing

  Identifying the purpose of and collecting relevant data to enable effective exchange of information in a planned, systematic and sensitive manner.

- Motivating

  Understanding and empathizing with the needs of others in order to tap into their motivational drives to ensure optimal contribution.

- Team-working

  Developing synergistic working relationships built on trust, sharing and openness.

Business acumen

- Marketing awareness

  Understanding basic marketing principles in order to set up a system to tap into customer needs and market moves.

- Financial awareness

  Understanding the concepts of profit and loss, cash flow and managing budgets in order to use financial information effectively.

- Statistical and analytical skill

  Gathering, collating, interpreting and using information.

- Strategic awareness

  Determining future possibilities through the use of broad creative flexible thought and understanding.

- Political sensitivity

   Recognizing and effectively balancing the interests and needs of one's own group with those of the broader organization. Understanding the agendas and perspectives of others.

- Helicoptering

   Rising above the detail of events, seeing the 'big picture' and the wider network of forces that are usually outside your influence.

- Visioning

   Communicating future possibilities through the use of words, pictures and imagery.

Now think about your own competences. The following exercise has been designed to assist you in reviewing your level of competence in each of the areas.

Exercise 26

COMPETENCE REVIEW

Think about each competence in terms of situations that occur across the major areas of your life, particularly work. Rate yourself using the following five-point scale:

Not competent	An unused and untested area, or where you are totally lacking
Some competence	A slight ability demonstrated in this area
Fairly competent	An average ability demonstrated in this area
Very competent	An above average ability demonstrated in this area
Extremely competent	Regarded as an expert in this area

	Not competent 1	*Some competence 2*	*Fairly competent 3*	*Very competent 4*	*Extremely competent 5*

INDIVIDUAL SKILLS

Controlling and managing yourself
Organizing yourself and channelling your energy towards productive ends. Keeping calm in stressful situations.

☐ ☐ ☐ ☐ ☐

Logical and critical thinking
Structuring your thoughts into rational frameworks, then using these for critical evaluation and analysing your own and others' ideas.

☐ ☐ ☐ ☐ ☐

Managing time
Allocating priorities, thinking through and making productive use of time available.

☐ ☐ ☐ ☐ ☐

Managing uncertainty and ambiguity
Being prepared to move away from familar ways of thinking and working, and dealing with uncertain situations comfortably.

☐ ☐ ☐ ☐ ☐

Creativity
Having a sense of originality and being able to imput new ideas. Arriving at new solutions to old problems.

☐ ☐ ☐ ☐ ☐

	Not competent 1	*Some competence 2*	*Fairly competent 3*	*Very competent 4*	*Extremely competent 5*

Self-confidence and assertiveness

Demonstrating a belief in yourself, and being able to express what you feel is right in social and work situations. Ultimately being able to say no when others want you to say yes.

☐ ☐ ☐ ☐ ☐

Communication – spoken and written

Expressing yourself clearly when talking to people, speaking at meetings, making formal and fluent presentations and writng effectively.

☐ ☐ ☐ ☐ ☐

Listening

Being attentive to people's views and ideas. Giving time and being patient in order to understand their concerns, feelings and interpretations on issues.

☐ ☐ ☐ ☐ ☐

Problem-solving and decision-making

Being able to think through and work with the diverse elements of a problem, then integrating the elements and making a decision.

☐ ☐ ☐ ☐ ☐

	Not competent 1	*Some competence 2*	*Fairly competent 3*	*Very competent 4*	*Extremely competent 5*

Self-development and learning
Taking responsibility and control
for your own development and
learning. Planning your future
direction.

☐ ☐ ☐ ☐ ☐

MANAGING RELATIONSHIPS

Performance management
Agreeing, monitoring and
achieving performance standards
and targets in key result areas.

☐ ☐ ☐ ☐ ☐

Networking
Identifying and building a cluster
of mutually beneficial
relationships and developing a
wide range of contacts.

☐ ☐ ☐ ☐ ☐

Delegating
Developing others by passing on
some of your authority and
responsibility for tasks in a
systematic way, thus giving you
time to take on more challenging
tasks from your boss.

☐ ☐ ☐ ☐ ☐

	Not competent 1	Some competence 2	Fairly competent 3	Very competent 4	Extremely competent 5

Influencing

Adapting behaviour and communication style to influence and gain commitment from people in a wide range of areas and at all levels.

☐ ☐ ☐ ☐ ☐

Handling others' difficulties

Helping others by acting as a counsellor, mentor and coach in order to assist in working through their personal difficulties.

☐ ☐ ☐ ☐ ☐

Interviewing

Identifying the purpose of and collecting relevent data to enable effective exchange of information in a planned, systematic and sensitive manner.

☐ ☐ ☐ ☐ ☐

Motivating

Understanding and empathizing with the needs of others in order to tap into their motivational drives to ensure optimal contribution.

☐ ☐ ☐ ☐ ☐

Team-working

Developing synergistic working relationships built on trust, sharing and openness.

☐ ☐ ☐ ☐ ☐

| | *Not competent 1* | *Some competence 2* | *Fairly competent 3* | *Very competent 4* | *Extremely competent 5* |

BUSINESS ACUMEN

Marketing awareness
Understanding basic marketing
principles in order to set up a
system to tap into customer
needs and market moves.

☐ ☐ ☐ ☐ ☐

Financial awareness
Understanding the concepts of
profit and loss, cash flow and
managing budgets in order to use
financial information effectively.

☐ ☐ ☐ ☐ ☐

Statistical and analytical skill
Gathering, collating, interpreting
and using information.

☐ ☐ ☐ ☐ ☐

Strategic awareness
Determing future possibilities
through the use of broad
creative flexible thought
and understanding.

☐ ☐ ☐ ☐ ☐

Political sensitivity
Recognizing and effectively
balancing the interests and needs
of one's own group with those of
the broader organization.
Understanding the agendas and
perspectives of others.

☐ ☐ ☐ ☐ ☐

	Not competent 1	Some competence 2	Fairly competent 3	Very competent 4	Extremely competent 5

Helicoptering

Rising above the detail of events, seeing the 'big picture' and the wider network of forces that are usually outside your influence.

| ☐ | ☐ | ☐ | ☐ | ☐ |

Visioning

Communicating future possibilities through the use of words, pictures and imagery.

| ☐ | ☐ | ☐ | ☐ | ☐ |

SUMMARY

What are your competences?

List those competences where you have marked yourself either very competent or extremely competent. Now reflect on why you marked yourself in this way by noting down the tangible achievements that led you to come to this conclusion:

Competence   *Tangible achievements*

_____   _____

_____   _____

_____   _____

_____   _____

_____   _____

Are any of the above competences either over- or under-used at the moment?

Over-used   *Under-used*

_____   _____

_____   _____

_____   _____

_____   _____

_____   _____

_____   _____

_____   _____

_____   _____

For example you may find it useful to note below those competences where you have marked yourself as less than very competent but which you feel you may need in the future.

_____

_____

_____

_____

_____

Note: This exercise is primarily designed for looking back over 'What you have done'. However it can also be useful in reviewing 'What you have learned' and 'Where you are going.'

In order to do things in the future we must build on what we have done in the past. Recalling what these events were is a vital part of this process. We may have a lot of things which we could use, that we may have temporarily forgotten. We need to have them to hand. After completing this milestone you should be well-armed for the journey still to come.

SUMMARY

In this milestone we have looked at what you have done in your life and we have explored and asked you to complete exercises in relation to:

- Timescales and your achievements
- Life and career stages
- Achievements in the different aspects of your life and in different roles
- Competences that you have and use.

MILESTONE 3

How did I learn?

Here we ask you to examine the way that you learn. In particular it is important to have an understanding of your preferred learning approaches. We also explore those 'accidental' learning experiences we have.

How can we discover how we learned to achieve the things that we have achieved? We can do it by relating to incidents in our past, in a variety of ways that will stimulate recall of events that we now know to be key. At the time they occurred they seemed to be not so significant; now, because we can recall them, we know that they must be.

The word 'learn' may suggest to you a formal setting. But we learn in a variety of situations, at a variety of paces and at differing times after the event, that precipitated or started the learning.

In terms of the content, there are three different types of learning. Firstly there is the kind that is focused upon pure facts or information, or knowledge and understanding. This has sometimes been called cognitive learning, and it occurs as a direct consequence of absorbing factual information that has immediate relevance, but does not have any great or long-term effect upon who the person is or what the person does. An example of this type might be you learning to understand the basic principles of a computer's operating system.

A second type would be learning a skill. You might learn how to present information in an interesting and comprehensible way; or you might learn how to make a golf or cricket ball swerve. You could learn how to operate a video camera, or reverse a tractor and trailer. Or you might learn how to produce simple spreadsheets on a computer.

A third type is to do with attitudes and realizations. You can learn to change your perception of the world or of yourself. You can learn to see yourself as others see you, to accept strengths of which you were unaware, to think of yourself as a parent or to be more objective when you think about a group of people to whom you have previously found it hard to relate. It is not situation-specific like the other two. It could be that you now feel confident enough to join in a discussion relating to computer spreadsheets.

So as you can see these are three different types of learning that you can use in a variety of situations. The question is – how did I learn and become what I am? Are there ways of learning that I could use now to help me achieve my present goals? How can I recall them? Are there learning opportunities that I am not at present taking?

Why do you need to ask these questions of yourself? Because, as well as discovering who you are, and what you have achieved, it will help you in your path to self-development if you can bring to the forefront of your consciousness, your awareness, how you learned to achieve, how you learned about yourself.

Are there any other reasons why you should undertake this challenging exercise? Of course there are! You tackle it in order to grow in ways that you want to so that you can control your growth yourself. Otherwise you may find that your growth may be random, or may even be controlling you.

This is an assertive phase of your planning. It is also an active phase, preparing for other actions. You need to have all aspects of your life under review and under control. This includes knowing how you have learned in the past, so that you can, when you want to, harness that way of learning for your future.

What we are suggesting that you do is indulge in a kind of creativity session. In creativity sessions you do not restrict your thoughts; you do not judge ideas to be useful or useless; you build on them, whatever they are, and explore around these areas, these ideas that occur to you. But starting the process, getting going, is often the hardest part. So here are some exercises that will help you to start motoring down the avenues of your past experience. These activities can be undergone alone, or in company. The advantage of being alone is that you will not be distracted if you have a tortuous path to follow, and faint memories to recall and hang on to. The advantage of company is that others may remind you of events in your own life, by some chance reference to theirs. They may also build on things that you mention, before passing them back for you to continue your adventurous drive into the memory cells.

CHILDHOOD REFLECTIONS

Let your mind wander to the earliest times that you can recall, or have been told about by your family and friends. Can you recall that first time that you felt embarrassment, and you learned about acceptable and unacceptable behaviours? You did it by observing human reactions. Sometimes you have since learned to ignore reactions to your behaviour. Would it be useful to become as sensitive again?

Can you recall pleasant moments, and what you did to influence these? You may have social skills that you have left untouched for aeons, but which could become accessible again, for present and future use.

Pass on to later childhood and repeat the process. You might recall the surprise that you experienced when you discovered that riding a tricycle on two wheels (tilted at an angle) could break the cheap metal axle between the two rear wheels if you could hold that position long enough. (You probably also found that your scientific discovery was not universally greeted with praise!)

Or consider the following case study:

Elizabeth, head of the computer department, was talking at work with friends from other departments over a post-lunchtime coffee. The conversation wandered on to the introduction of the new software system, and the fact that in some of the training sessions some staff members were very ill-at-ease with the positions of their keyboards. The conversation then turned to causes of repetitive strain injuries. Elizabeth told her colleagues her theories about people getting it because they only moved their hands and fingers, and not their arms and wrists. She said that she could not sit with her arms resting on the table because her piano teacher had always encouraged her to prance her hands over the keys, and to move them up and down like the legs of a cantering horse. She still did this, both while playing the piano and using the computer keyboard. So, she became aware that her training as a pianist had multiple uses.

One way of doing this reflection is to use time that would otherwise be wasted, so start practising this recall when you find yourself waiting, and cannot do anything else productive. For instance, when you are early for an appointment at the dentist's; or when you are being driven on a familiar journey, or waiting at an airport. Try it if you cannot drop off to sleep one night, and so on. It will help to have a medium for recall available, whether it is electronic (tape, video recorder or laptop) or simply a notepad and pen.

Exercise 27

MY CHILDHOOD REFLECTIONS

Now let your mind wander back to your own childhood reflections and note them down.

_____

_____

_____

_____

_____

Go back to your notes and read them through again. What further events do they remind you of? What things need to be unlearned because they are now no longer relevant to you as an adult? What permissions can you give yourself, in order to open up possibilities that you have, up to now, considered to be beyond your reach?

_____

_____

_____

_____

_____

Consider the following case.

Julie, as a child, denied herself the opportunity to take on roles of responsibility when asked by others (e.g. school prefect) since she felt it was presumptuous. Now, as a professional woman, she positively accepts that taking advantage of certain opportunities when offered can indeed be beneficial and developmental.

Make three lists of these events.

Further reflections

Things to be unlearned

List of new things to try in the future

_____	_____	_____
_____	_____	_____
_____	_____	_____
_____	_____	_____
_____	_____	_____

Now for another memory jogger. This is called serendipity. According to the Concise Oxford Dictionary, (eighth edition, 1990), this is 'The faculty of making happy and unexpected discoveries by accident'. A more down to earth definition might be 'Discovering things by falling over them, when attempting to find something else'. The term was first used by Horace Walpole in 1754, but he formed it from the title of the Sri Lankan fairy tale *The Three Princes of Serendip.*

To play Serendipity try to recall times when you intended to do one thing, but found yourself having done another. It may help to look at some examples. If not, move on to Exercise 28: Serendipity.

John went to buy a new kettle, but could not find one that he liked. However, he saw a wok at a bargain price, and learnt Chinese cookery in order to put his 'bargain' to good use. Although he had never cooked before, he found he took to it easily, and later the social skills that he had developed at evening class helped him in his relationships with others, which up to then he had never found easy. It also improved his confidence that as an adult, he could still learn new tricks en route, or even en croute!

Jane joined the Debating Society at college because she quite fancied someone she knew to be a member. To her surprise she found that debating was an easy skill to learn. She had always had a logical mind and soon found herself debating in the fourth team. After two years she was in the team that won the Observer Mace, the highest honour. In later years, as a manager, she found that she was good at putting forward credible arguments, not just in meetings, but in reports. This aided her bid for promotion to a position where a need for accurate reports was at the heart of the job. (This is an example of what we might call Extended Serendipity. The effect took place over a longer timescale, and was not a probable outcome in Jane's teenage scenario.)

Bob had to listen to two sermons each Sunday. To prevent boredom, he elected to pick holes in the arguments of the preachers. He became quite expert in detecting the flaws in their arguments, and this skill proved very useful in Union and Management negotiations years later, when he became Human Resource Manager for his company.

Karen was put in charge of her netball team as she was the largest child. She found that others in her team listened to her and enjoyed the fact that their team performances improved. They came from being an easy team to beat to one that was a match for even the toughest opponents. This gave her confidence in controlling staff through team leadership when she became a supervisor. In fact, she claimed that supervising in an office context was easier that captaining her netball team!

Elaine sang in an Irish folk club, and Charles in a Methodist choir. From being shy in the background in the chorus of their respective choirs when young, they rose to be soloists. Both now have voices that command attention in their work situations.

Exercise 28

SERENDIPITY

Think of things that you learned which could now have a use, perhaps formatted in a different way. Go over your home, school, and early employment experiences to think of things that you learned accidentally when doing something else.

Make sure you record how you learned them. We will be looking at preferred learning styles later in this section.

_____

_____

_____

_____

_____

What you have been doing here is to think of transferable achievements – things that could aid you now and in the future, even if they have been unused for many years. You can also think of things that could transfer from the context of a hobby, pastime, or social or domestic areas into your area of work.

Transferable achievements

_____

_____

_____

_____

_____

What to do next

Write down all the skills or abilities that you have which you or others consider are unusual: things that could be used in your future journeys, even if, at the moment, it is not clear how this could be.

Unusual skills or abilities

_____

_____

_____

_____

_____

_____

Significant learning experiences

Another way to improve your future is to try to recall events that were significant learning experiences for you. These events might have lasted for seconds, minutes, hours, or even days, weeks, months or years. Consider why it was a significant event, how it happened to you and what it taught you. Do you believe that what you learned is helpful now? Have new ways of applying what you learned occurred to you since? Think about how you learned as well as what you learned, and what you liked about the process and the outcome.

Exercise 29

MY MOST SIGNIFICANT LEARNING EXPERIENCES

(and my feelings and thoughts about them)

_____

_____

_____

_____

_____

_____

_____

_____

_____

_____

SEGMENTING YOUR LEARNING

People sometimes assume that they learn different kinds of things in different environments – so let's find out if this is true for you.

Exercise 30

SEGMENTING MY LEARNING

List all the different environments that you have learned from in the past. If the list contains six or less, allocate a number between one and six to each. For instance, the environments could be: School, home, college, youth club, work (temporary and full time), interest areas (films, music) or any area that occupied a significant amount of your time.

_____

_____

_____

_____

_____

_____

Take a die and throw it. Each time it lands relate the number shown to a learning segment. The challenge is to remember one example of how you learned from that environment and record it. Only when you have listed some event can you move on and throw the die again.

This exercise could prove to be quite challenging, and we feel you may find it more beneficial and fun to do this in a small group. Of course, it is also possible to do this on your own. If you come up with more than six, but less than thirteen areas, you can use two dice.

Area 1

_____

_____

_____

_____

_____

Area 2

_____

_____

_____

_____

_____

Area 3

_____

_____

_____

_____

_____

Area 4

_____

_____

_____

_____

_____

Area 5

_____

_____

_____

_____

_____

Area 6

_____

_____

_____

_____

_____

Look to see if you have similarities in the ways that you prefer to learn across these areas that you have identified. If there seems to be a pattern, it may be that you can focus on that type of learning for best future results. Conversely, it may be that other ways of learning which you have not used so far, could be tried, and might produce different or even better ways for you to absorb knowledge and skills.

STYLES OF LEARNING

If you find that you experience some difficulty in deciding your own categories for learning styles, you may find it useful to 'borrow' a model of learning styles from someone else. For instance David Kolb has a four-way categorization of learning styles that has also been adapted by Peter Honey and Alan Mumford.

There are four styles that can be used. These styles could be thought of as combining to form a four-stage cycle. First there is the concrete experience (CE), followed by reflecting and observing (RO); this leads to building up abstract concepts and generalizations (AC) followed by testing of hypotheses and the implications of these concepts (AE). This takes us round to the beginning of the cycle again.

 Exercise 31

MY LEARNING STYLE

Below are set out some words arranged near the initials of the style of learning that they represent. Now tick any words that relate to the way in which you learn. Tick as many of these words as you like.

```
                    CE
                  Tuned-in
                   Aware
                  Believing
Realistic          Knowing          Distant
Experimental      Experience         Seeing
Active             Sensing           Viewing
AE ─────────────────────────────────── RO
Down-to-earth     Systematic        Reflecting
Testing          Digging deep       Observing
Practical         Thorough          Attentive
                   Logical
                  Thinking
                  Cerebral
                    AC
```

Now add up the number of words that you have ticked in the **CE** column, and circle that number where it appears on the score sheet under **CE**. Repeat this for the other three areas.

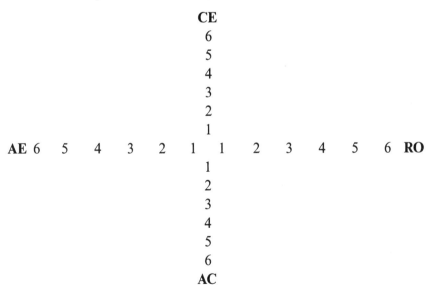

```
                      CE
                      6
                      5
                      4
                      3
                      2
                      1
AE 6   5   4   3   2   1   1   2   3   4   5   6  RO
                      1
                      2
                      3
                      4
                      5
                      6
                      AC
```

Now connect each point to the two on either side of it, so that you generate/produce a four-sided shape. This gives you a rough indication of your preferences for each style against the others.

You probably use all four methods, but over- or under-use some of them at times. Or perhaps you use them out of sequence. It makes sense to use them together, and in a cycle, perhaps starting with checking out your past experiences, reflecting on them and on the present state of your skill or knowledge, getting a handle on the big picture, and then trying it out for real.

This generates some more concrete experiences, and so then you are ready to go round the cycle again. You could start at any place on the cycle, and managers from different cultures tend to start in different places. For instance in an Anglo-French joint venture, we found that the French managers preferred to start with Abstract Conceptualization, and the British with Active Experimentation or Concrete Experience.

If you pay too little or too much attention to the past it will impair your learning by constraining you from using or even considering new ideas and new ways of doing things. If you spend too little time looking back you may be re-discovering the wheel, or forgetting some huge leap forward. Similarly, if you spend all your time actively experimenting, and never pause to reflect on what has been happening, you will not learn well from your active experimentation. You can follow this logic for all areas in the learning cycle.

It is sometimes said that there is tension or conflict between concrete experience and abstract conceptualization, and that if one is used a lot, then the other will be used little; similarly for reflective observation and active experimentation, if you constantly reflect you will not do much testing out of hypotheses. But this in turn depends upon whether you have generated hypotheses to be tested!

In practice we have found people with many variations of the profile, reflecting variations in learning preferences. Some have profiles that are high on both **CE** and **AC** but low on **AE** and

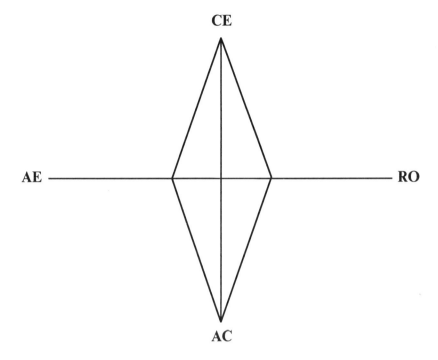

Fig 4.1 Learning style profile 1

RO. (see Fig 4.1); others have profiles high on **AE** and **RO** but low on **CE** and **AC** (see Fig 4.2).

Many organizations are encouraging managers to follow a mentoring approach at the moment. If you have not used one before, try to identify someone who could act in this way for you, and either approach them yourself, if you already know them, or find someone who knows you both, to make the first move.

We have found that choosing mentors for others is not as satisfactory as encouraging people to find their own. If you feel this is a daunting prospect, enlist help. You need someone that you can open up to, and a person who is not too directive. What you need is a reflector, someone with some non-directive coaching skills available. The model of coaching demonstrated by David

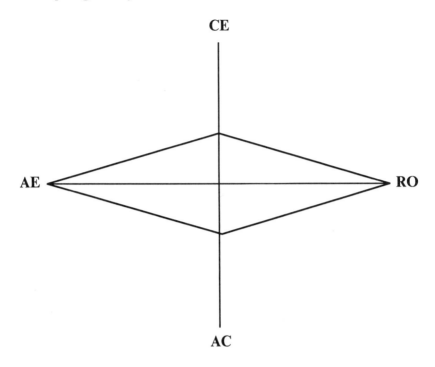

Fig 4.2 Learning style profile 2

Whitaker, Dr David Hemery and Sir John Whitmore in their 'Coaching for Performance' videos is ideal. They say that the best, most effective way to coach is not to tell, but to ask. Ask people what matters to them, what concerns they have and what issues are they interested in, in order to focus their mind. Then, follow their interest, not your agenda. Start broad and then narrow the focus. Ask, listen and reflect. Repeat their words back to them. Generate responsibility, that is, hand it over to them and do not fall for the temptation to lead them, force your own agenda on them, or push for solutions that you think will work.

So for you, the self-managed developer, the process means not allowing a coach or mentor to tell you what to do. You do not need someone who is motivated by showing you how good they are, or how much they know. As in any change process you will not be committed unless you have ownership and total involvement. This is your process. You are the only one who can decide how to learn, and what to learn. Ordinary people that you have known in other circumstances such as work, sport, pastimes, interests, hobbies, could also help if you have the courage to approach them, listen to them, and try to absorb what they have to tell you.

Most people claim to want feedback, but are often (naturally enough) defensive if it is not all positive, or if it is not fed back in a constructive or skilful way. However in the context of your long journey it is worth while biting your tongue sometimes so that the flow of information continues. You need to be honest with yourself, if you want to gain useful knowledge from these sources.

In preparing for the next stages in your journey you need to understand how you operate, and particularly how you can best take on board new information, knowledge and skills, that better prepare you (possibly!) for the arduous travels ahead.

 Exercise 32

MY LEARNING REVIEW

Write down the most important messages coming from your examination of your learning experiences.

_____

_____

_____

_____

SUMMARY

Looking back, then, in this milestone you have:

- Reflected back to learning experiences in your past and examined them for any patterns of recurring approaches to learning or indeed things you have avoided
- Thought about accidental learning experiences and their meaning for you
- Identified your most significant learning experiences
- Examined the concept of learning styles and identified your own preferred style.

Finally we suggested that as well as considering your own views about learning you should also get feedback from others.

MILESTONE 4

Where am I going?

'If you don't know where you are going you will probably end up somewhere else.'
DR L. J. PETER

It is now time to begin planning *where* you want to go. In this milestone we encourage you to do a bit of dreaming in terms of both your life and career. We also examine and suggest how to set and decide upon your objectives. We also recognize that to be realistic in this area diversions will have to be navigated along the route.

The final part of 'Preparing the way' is to enable you to be very clear on your precise destination. It is at this point that you are required to look in the direction of the future and speculate about what route you intend to take. It is possibly the least tangible of all the parts of 'Preparing the way' because it has not happened yet; so it is always subject to modification and change.

When thinking about future destinations there are people who set themselves fairly simple, straightforward objectives and therefore have a relatively short journey. Alternatively there are those who have wild imaginations and are always dreaming about what is clearly an unattainable end – they have a long or uncompleted journey. In our experience the size of the journey is not the most important factor. The degree of success individuals have in reaching their destinations is largely dependent upon their clarity of vision about where they are going. This section is designed to clear away the fog, mist and other distractions, giving *you* greater clarity of vision.

By now you will probably have a very good idea of whether you are the sort of person who embarks upon straightforward journeys, or those that never come to an end. For the purposes of the first exercise we suggest that you assume the personality of the dreamer.

Exercise 33

MY IDEAL WORLD

Thinking about your ideal life or career is usually the sort of activity that is frowned upon by a society which encourages people to become deeply rooted in reality. Just for once here is an opportunity to remove all of the usual blocks associated with age, health, money, time, etc. and let your mind wander.

In the order which is comfortable for you, consider both your 'ideal career' and in a broader context your 'ideal life'. When thinking about your 'ideal career' start where you are now and explore issues such as income, status, work/home balance, the sorts of tasks you enjoy doing, and the sorts of opportunities for further development this career-path will bring. In your 'ideal life' scenario you might want to paint a picture that brings together all the different facets of your life (work, home and social) in a more integrated way. Be creative. You now have a blank sheet of paper.

My 'ideal career'

_____

_____

_____

_____

_____

My 'ideal life'

_____

_____

_____

_____

_____

Now that you have recorded these two particular ideals it is important to take them a stage further by addressing the following questions:

What do they tell you about your values and aspirations?

Career   *Life*

_____   _____

_____   _____

_____   _____

_____   _____

Is there a big difference between your ideal and reality? If so, is any of your ideal achievable?

Career   *Life*

_____   _____

_____   _____

_____   _____

_____   _____

_____   _____

What are the barriers to getting closer to your ideal?

Career   *Life*

_____   _____

_____   _____

_____   _____

_____   _____

Summarize your thinking by positioning your ideal scenarios as either pure fantasy or as something that gives you a set of broad objectives which could be taken further and worked on.

_____

_____

_____

_____

SETTING OBJECTIVES ALONG THE WAY

For those of you who are used either to conducting or being on the receiving end of appraisal interviews at work, the term 'objective setting' may be familiar. The following simple steps adequately describe the process for setting your objectives:

- Define the areas where results are expected from the job – key result areas.
- Define what can be measured in these areas – performance indicators.
- Define the specific targets to be achieved – your objectives.

Take the following example from a customer service manager's job:

Key result area: *Customer complaints*

Performance indicator: *Weekly complaints per product*

Objective: *To reduce customer complaints by 10% in the next 12 months*

Most objectives can be distinguished by referring to them as either 'hard' or 'soft'. Hard objectives are usually easy to quantify as in the example above, whereas soft objectives usually refer to the qualitative way in which a job is carried out, and are much less easy to quantify – e.g. improving your assertiveness techniques when engaged in conflict. The guidelines that follow are equally applicable to both sorts of objectives.

When thinking about and creating objectives for yourself it is useful to put them within a framework that allows you the greatest possible chance of reaching them. A well tried and trusted framework is to apply the **SMART** technique. With each objective you need to ask yourself the following questions:

S Is it specific enough? Objectives should state clearly how much, how well, at what cost, within what degree of accuracy, compared to what?

M Is it measurable, giving me some sort of gauge as to how much progress I am making? This is obviously easier for some jobs than for others; but even for service-oriented jobs (always difficult to quantify) it is often possible to identify some valid performance indicators on which objectives can be based.

A Is it sufficiently action oriented? In other words, during the process of moving from where I am now to some future position, are there some concrete things I need to do?

R Is it realistic enough to make it both challenging and attainable? Good objectives are always stretching, challenging and developmental – particularly when you set them yourself. However, unattainable objectives can be extremely demotivating.

T Does it have a time frame around it? Essentially you need to know by what date a particular objective needs to be achieved. Somewhat related to this – if your job situation changes, making the objective significantly more or less achievable, the objective should be reviewed and updated.

When setting objectives for yourself it is easy to get enthusiastic and set too many. This creates a situation where your attention is easily diluted and your focus lost. There is no universally 'correct' number of course; this will vary from job to job and person to person. When in doubt try to aim for fewer rather than more.

When thinking about your own specific objectives the following list of questions is a useful prompt:

- What is my objective?
- What are the consequences of not achieving this objective?
- What are the conflicting objectives?
- Why is this objective important?
- What are the obstacles to meeting my objective?
- What internal and external resources are available?
- What are my operational strategies?
- What sacrifices will have to be made (mine and others)?

● What are my time frames?
● How will I measure my progress?

Consider the following typical example of a work-based specific objective.

Objective	*To be more assertive in meetings at work.*
Consequences of not achieving objective	*My ideas will continue to be rejected. My self-confidence will suffer.*
Conflicting objectives	*I like to be liked. Becoming more pushy might make me unpopular*
Why this objective is important	*A criterion for further promotion is to show that I have ideas. I have ideas, but others get in before me. I lose out while they take all the credit.*
Obstacles	*Personality characteristics such as shyness, lack of confidence and an unwillingness to appear pushy.*
Available internal and external resources	*Assertiveness training programmes. Possibility of working on it together with a like-minded colleague who has a similar problem. My partner, who is always willing to offer personal perspectives on these sorts of issues.*

Operational strategies

Get ideas from other people. Make all the necessary planning before a meeting – what to say, how and when to say it. Make a short contribution at my next meeting and increase the contributions little by little at subsequent meetings.

Sacrifices (myself and others)

I will have to sacrifice the feeling of wanting to be liked by everyone. Allocating preparation time before meetings will have time management implications. My partner may have to suffer some added pressures while I adapt to this new way of operating.

Time frames

I will start the process next week and be making a significant impact at meetings within 6 months.

Measuring processes

When preparing for meetings I will note down my objective for that particular meeting and monitor the outcome myself. I will also ask several of my colleagues to monitor my progress and give me formal feedback at regular quarterly intervals.

One of the greatest dangers when setting objectives is to leave an objective hanging in mid-air because you don't really know how to progress it at all. In order to begin the process of making your objectives come to life, take an objective and subject it to the criteria outlined in the acronym **SMART.** This will assist you in the early stages of your thinking when developing some broad guidelines and boundaries. Now try and be more specific about each objective by using the format outlined below.

Exercise 34

SETTING MY OBJECTIVES

Objective(s)

_____

_____

_____

_____

_____

Consequences of **not** *achieving objective*

_____

_____

_____

_____

_____

Conflicting objectives

_____

_____

_____

_____

Why this objective is important

_____

_____

_____

_____

Obstacles

_____

_____

_____

_____

Available internal and external resources

_____

_____

_____

_____

Operational strategies

_____

_____

_____

_____

Sacrifices (myself and others)

_____

_____

_____

_____

Time frames

_____

_____

_____

_____

Measuring processes

_____

_____

_____

_____

POTENTIAL DIVERSIONS

You may be starting to get the impression that setting your objectives and then starting out on the road to reach them is a fairly straightforward sort of journey. If it was that simple people would regularly set themselves lots of objectives, reach them, then go through the process of setting themselves more. Clearly it does not happen that way. You will probably set out with lots of good intentions and then get distracted. It is highly unlikely that your schedule will allow you to devote all (or even most) of your time and energy to reaching your stated objectives. Life is just not like that!

If you expect and prepare for some possible diversions then you will probably be in a better position to be able to deal with them. Before focusing on some of the specific aspects of those things that might divert you and what you might do to alleviate or remove them completely, consider the broad issues and complete the following exercise.

 Exercise 35

POTENTIAL DIVERSIONS

Consider the things that might divert you from reaching your objectives.

Things about me (e.g. personality characteristics, lack of skills)

_____

_____

_____

_____

Things about those around me (e.g. competitive elements, cultural factors)

_____

_____

_____

_____

Things about my personal needs (e.g. family and environmental needs)

_____

_____

_____

_____

Things about the organization for which I work (e.g. openness, opportunities)

_____

_____

_____

_____

Things about the nature of my work (e.g. mundane, no challenge, too busy)

_____

_____

_____

_____

Things about my preferred lifestyle (e.g. hours I want to work)

_____

_____

_____

_____

Conflicts between home and work (e.g. time allocation, reloca-tion possibilities)

_____

_____

_____

_____

Other factors

_____

_____

_____

_____

DYNAMICS IN SETTING OBJECTIVES

Now that you have some broad ideas about those things that might get in your way it will be useful to build on these ideas and engage in what psychologists refer to as 'Force-field analysis'. This is a simple technique designed to improve your chances of achieving an objective. In this instance it allows you to examine what is involved in making the changes necessary to reach your objective. In addition to this it has the added benefit of helping you to get a sense of proportion about the negative factors and influences that might get in your way. The technique revolves around the notion that in any situation where change is desired there will always be some forces at work that are acting with you and some forces working against you.

Before working on your own 'force-field' consider the following brief case study.

Brian was the manager of a well-known department store. In his appraisal interview with the Regional Director he set himself a major objective for the following year – to empower his team of section heads. Because the business and many of the team (including himself) were in a rut (represented by the Equilibrium State line shown in Fig 5.1) Brian felt that the time had come for quite drastic measures. To Brian, 'empowerment' meant giving the section heads a greater say in their everyday working lives – particularly in the area of decision-making. This is the Ideal State line shown in Fig 5.1. He knew that some of his team would welcome this change and also that there were likely to be some who would resist it. A particular concern was the degree to which this branch would be moving away from the operating culture of the other regional branches and how Head Office would view this.

Diagrammatically the forces working for and against Brian's objective look something like Fig 5.2.

In dealing with these forces Brian might be continually tempted to give added momentum to the driving forces in order to move towards his 'ideal state'. However the model is dynamic because if the forces are increased in one direction, then the forces in the opposite direction (the resisting forces) must increase equally if the equilibrium is to be maintained. The net effect of this approach would be to increase the over-all tension.

This approach to change is rather like trying to stop a car by using the brakes, without taking one's foot off the accelerator. If at the same time as adding momentum to his driving forces Brian tackles one or other of the resisting forces, he opens up the possibility of achieving a new equilibrium (e.g. the 'ideal state') but at a lower level of tension.

The Force-field analysis exercise invites you to plot, analyse, and action one or more of your objectives as a means of achieving real change.

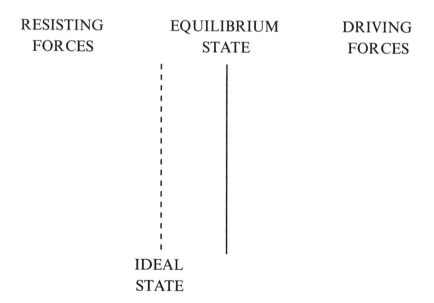

Fig 5.1 Force-field analysis diagram

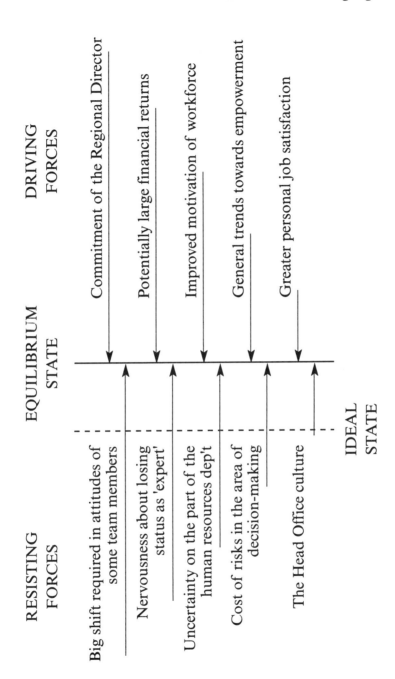

Fig 5.2 Force-field analysis (Brian's objective)

Exercise 36

MY FORCE-FIELD ANALYSIS

To use this technique successfully you need to work through the following five important stages.

1 Creating a vision of your ideal outcome

Take one of your objectives and try to paint a mental picture of what your ideal outcome would look like. Adopt a way of thinking that lies somewhere between the determination involved in setting a clear objective and the imagination involved in a pleasant day-dream. If necessary assist the process by:

- asking yourself some 'what if' questions such as: 'what if time were no object?' or 'what if I had unlimited resources?'
- projecting yourself into the future and trying to imagine what you are saying and doing
- suppressing blocking thoughts such as 'it will never work' or 'it is only a dream'.

_____

_____

_____

_____

2 Listing and weighting the resisting forces

Now set them free and allow the fears, doubts and worries to sur-face as resisting forces. Try to analyse and scale each resisting force in order to be clear about its relative significance as compared with others. Put in rank order the resisting forces so that you can distinguish between those that are major stumbling blocks and those that might be easiest to remove.

_____

_____

_____

3 Listing and weighting the driving forces

In much the same way as you proceeded in the previous step, think about, and put in rank order, those things that will be working in your favour. Maybe it will be useful to recall things that you listed and thought about in the section called 'What have I done'. Internal personality characteristics such as your own motivation might be hard to specify and rank. List them and try to weight the relative importance of all the driving forces.

_____

_____

_____

4 Produce a force-field analysis diagram

Refer to the example illustrated earlier (see Figs 5.1 and 5.2) as guidance. Remember :

Centre line = Equilibrium state (where you are now)
Dotted line = Ideal state (where you would like to be)
Arrows to left and right = Resisting and driving forces

The size of the arrow represents the weighting of the force operating i.e. the bigger the arrow, the more significant the force.

5 Identify your areas of change

Under normal circumstances the most effective way of achieving movement is to begin by addressing the smallest resisting
force. As stated earlier if you start by putting more energy into
your driving forces you may generate more resistance. Exactly
where you start and how much energy you apply is a subjective
judgement that you are best qualified to make.

Before you actually start acting on your forces be clear about
the fact that your actions will be mainly dependent upon the
nature of the force you are dealing with combined with your
own ways of doing things. Try to remember that movement in
the situation is important for two main reasons:

- As the model is dynamic, movement in one force will often
  result in movement in others. For example, some of your
  opponents may not believe that your proposed change has
  much chance of success until they see some movement; at
  which point they may well reduce some of their resistance.
- It will help if you recognize your successes, however small.
  Gain encouragement from them and reward yourself. Given
  that your own energy is probably an important factor in the
  situation anything you can do to encourage yourself will be
  extremely beneficial.

SUMMARY

So looking back over this section 'Where am I going?' you have:

- Considered your ideal world scenarios
- Examined techniques of looking at your objectives

- Focused on your specific objectives
- Taken account of possible diversions to meeting your objectives
- Summarized the positive and negative factors attributable to a specific objective and explored ways of dealing with them.

We hope you are now ready to begin the more concrete business of 'Travelling the way'.

Stage 3

TRAVELLING
THE WAY

'Achieving good performance is a journey,
not a destination'.

In this final stage of our book we look at a variety of techniques for action planning, including contingency planning and coping strategies. We suggest some tips for keeping on track, but most of all we hope that by this stage you are truely committed to the concept of self-managed development and are ready to continue on your 'journey of discovery'.

The whole process of self-managed development hinges to a large extent on your own motivation to move forward and plan the way ahead. The process of getting started involved you in thinking about and exploring who you are, what you have done, how you learned and where you are going. We hope that by this stage you are now wondering how you are going to continue to 'travel the way'.

Many of the exercises in the earlier part of this book should have helped you to understand the various approaches, techniques, and experiences that helped you to learn and develop. Indeed, as well as the how you may also be beginning to focus on the what. Or put another way, you may be beginning to focus on the direction or maybe directions in which you wish to go. It is our hope that by this stage in the book you should be excited about what you have discovered about yourself and the richness and variety of experiences that go together to make you the person you are today. We also hope that you are itching to make use of this new-found knowledge not only by recognizing development opportunities for what they are but also by actively taking responsibility for travelling the way ahead in a direction planned by you.

MOVING ON

If you are to take advantage of the discoveries you have made while 'preparing the way', and if you wish to continue to explore as yet undiscovered territories, this next phase of the process of self-managed development is vital. In terms of how we go about this stage, much will depend upon our own idiosyncratic way of working.

If, for example, we are planning a car journey to a previously unvisited destination, most of us will need to refer to a road atlas. For some of us this reference will simply be a quick look to ascertain the general direction in which to travel and to get an idea of the location of our destination. Having this information we can then follow the relevant road signs and use our own intuitive sense of direction. At the other end of the spectrum, others will spend many hours pouring over the atlas planning the journey in detail, possibly even writing down the road numbers on which intend to travel. In both cases the journey may involve detours and the unexpected. In the former these detours will be treated as events to be dealt with along the way. In the latter the detours will have been planned into the journey in order to make it more worth while, and should anything unexpected happen, for instance a traffic jam, the plan is likely to be so exact that an alternative route will be easily taken.

So by analogy, just as you all have your own approaches to learning, you all have your own approach to planning. In this section as with all of the others you must choose what suits you best in terms of the approach you wish to employ for 'travelling the way'. Some of you will like to have lots of detail in your plan and even make contingency plans just in case! Others of you will simply wish to set an objective, perhaps with some indication of time or quality standards, but little detail of the route you are going to take along the way.

Exercise 37

MY SELF-MANAGED DEVELOPMENT OBJECTIVES

In order to focus your mind you may wish to start this section of the book by summarizing the key objectives you have set yourself so far as a result of the 'Where am I going' section. So start by listing your objectives and deciding whether they are short-, medium-, or long-term objectives. This will help you later on in the actual process of action planning.

My self-managed development objectives   *Timescale: S/M/L*

_____   _____

_____   _____

_____   _____

_____   _____

_____   _____

_____   _____

_____   _____

As we said at the beginning of this book the important thing for us is that you take responsibility for your own development. Part of that involves believing in and then adopting your own approach. We also believe that in order to move forward a vital element of your approach is having a well-defined plan. Someone once said 'If you aim at nothing you will sure as hell hit it'! For us, having a plan gives you something clear to aim at and while you may not always hit the bull's-eye, you should at least hit the target!

So, in this final chapter, we will be looking at various ways of action planning aiming to leave you at the crossroads ready to take whichever direction you choose in your journey of discovery.

We will also examine how to deal with detours and road-blocks, in other words contingency plans or coping strategies. No matter how organized you are it is almost inevitable that from time to time 'the best laid plans of mice and men gang aft aglee' (Burns). So we will look at how you get back onto the route you planned, and how you make best use of the detour.

Finally we will look at different ways of keeping track of where you are going.

PLANNING THE ROUTE

As we have already stated, there are many different approaches to action planning, and finding the right one for you is the most important issue. We believe that by taking more responsibility for your own development and by taking control, the next stage is to commit yourself to doing something. Often by writing something down the commitment is more solid than if it were simply committed to memory. For instance how many times have you said something like this to yourself 'I must brush up on my French before I go on my summer holidays' and the day before you go you are still packing the phrase book and still thinking 'I really should have spent some time brushing up'!

We are not suggesting that simply by writing something down you will do it but if you are truly committed to self-managed development and you have seriously thought through where you want to go then having an action plan should help you continue your journey. You may also wish to consider at this stage the number of different action plans you can tackle at any one time. You may wish to split them into short-, medium-, and long-term plans – perhaps with more detailed plans for the short-term – but over time, the medium- and long-term plans will become the short- and medium-term plans, thus perpetuating the 'never ending journey' concept.

So, in the action planning phase of self-managed development there are a number of questions you may wish to ask yourself before deciding the particular approach you wish to take at any one time:

- How easy or difficult will the goals be to achieve?
- How detailed does my plan have to be?
- Is this plan for short-, medium-, or long-term objectives?
- Are other people involved in my plan?
- How likely am I to reach roadblocks and detours along the way?
- How knowledgable am I of the subject area?

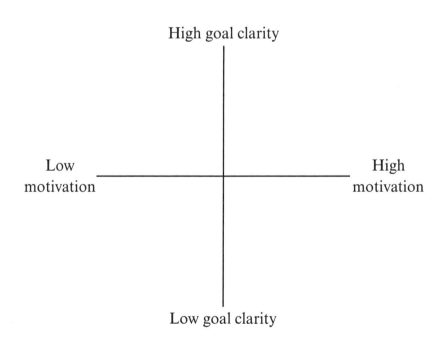

Fig 6.1 Goal clarity vs. motivation

- Do I need to share my plan with anyone else?
- How clear are the goals?
- How motivated am I to achieve the goals?

In trying to determine which goals to focus on first, or indeed which are the most important to focus on, you may find it useful to examine some of the above questions diagrammatically and in terms of two axes. It is possible to take two questions at a time, apply them to each goal and plot your answer on a chart – thus giving yourself the opportunity to compare and contrast several goals at one time before making final decisions about your priorities for action planning.

For instance, you may like to compare goal clarity with motivation to achieve (see Fig 6.1).

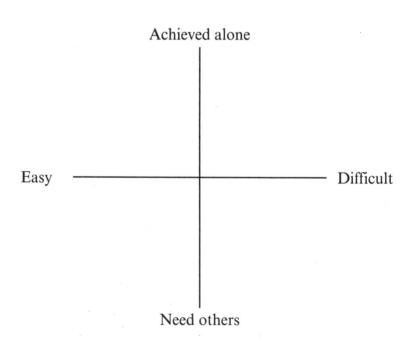

Fig 6.2 Others' involvement vs. ability to achieve

You should now consider each of your goals and plot them (using a code to identify each one) on the chart. In making your decision regarding priority those goals located in the top right-hand box are probably the most important to focus on in the first instance. Those in the bottom right hand box are also important but might require a little more work to ensure greater clarity.

Things to do	Deadline date

Fig 6.3 Action plan 1

Objective	Steps to take	Timescale

Fig 6.4 Action plan 2

Objective & timescale	Things going for me	Things going against me
People involved	**Resources necessary**	**Steps to take**

Fig 6.5 Action plan 3

You may also wish to compare ease of achievement with ability to achieve alone, or with others' assistance (see Fig 6.2). In examining this chart you may wish to ask yourself whether or not the relevant people are available to help you. Sometimes it helps motivation if you first tackle something easy you are in full control of, to get some success under your belt, before moving on to more difficult and complex issues.

These two-by-two boxes are very easy to create, and now that you are familiar with how to use them, you should create them to assist you in determining your goal priority list.

All these questions together with your own natural preferences in terms of action planning approach will have a bearing on the type of action plan you choose.

Things to do	Deadline date
• Learn new computer system	October 1994
• Write an article on self-managed development	July 1994
• Get more experience working overseas	Ongoing
• Gain experience working with other business units	December 1994
• Get fit and lose weight	Ongoing
• Learn holiday spanish	July 1995

Fig 6.6 Action plan 1 (example 1)

Things to do	Timescale
Learn new computer system • Enquire about training programmes • Select most appropriate programme • Enrol on programme • Practise keyboard skills • Work through various exercises • Begin to integrate with real work • Explore advanced techniques	October 1994

Fig 6.7 Action plan 1 (example 2)

At its simplest you may choose to adopt a 'to do list' (Fig 6.3) that can help you meet your needs in achieving a short-term goal where very little detail is needed and where you are relatively

Objective	Steps to take	Timescale
Keep fit	• Swim (20 lengths)	Weekly
	• Aerobic exercise (30 min)	2 × a week
	• Walk up stairs at office	All the time
	• Cycle to paper shop	Sundays
Lose weight (target weight 10st)	• Find suitable diet	End of week
	• Cut out chocolate bars	All the time
	• Eat less fat and dairy produce	All the time
	• Weigh self	Fortnightly

Fig 6.8 Action plan 2 (example)

knowledgable of the subject area.

For instance an example of a 'to do list' type of action plan might look like Fig 6.6.

Another simple action plan that involves three stages (see Fig 6.4) may be most appropriate for plans for which you require very little detail, possibly long-term plans or those where you are fairly knowledgable of the topic area.

At the other end of the spectrum a more detailed action plan (Fig 6.5) for the more complex objectives – perhaps where more people are involved in the process, or where your knowledge of the area is scant, thus requiring you to be more detailed in your planning process – might take this format.

In your approach to action planning there may well be a place for each of the above types of action planning.

Action Plan 1 (Fig 6.6) could be used to list all your objectives over a fairly long period as a checklist of your achievements. Or it

Objective & timescale	Things going for me	Things going against me
• Gain experience working overseas by December 1994	• The organization's international reputation • Previous experience • Opportunities available	• Lack of time • Competitive marketing • No foreign languages
People involved	**Resources necessary**	**Steps to take**
• Boss • Colleagues • Clients • Family	• Contacts • Budget • Information about countries and events	• Identify possible opportunity • Discuss with relevent people • Market sclf • Plan into diary

Fig 6.9 Action plan 3 (example)

could be used as a very simple action plan in meeting one of your objectives, for instance as in Fig 6.7.

Action Plan 2 (Fig 6.8) could be used where to meet one large objective you need to meet a variety of smaller objectives. You may fill up one sheet just by listing all the smaller objectives that you need to meet in order to fulfil your main objective.

Action Plan 3 (Fig 6.9) would be used in order to get to grips with an objective that requires more detailed planning, where you have little knowledge or skill of the area in question.

You may of course already have a well-designed, tried and tested approach to your own action planning that can be easily adapted for self-managed development. In line with our earlier messages the important thing is for you to find an approach that suits you and then to use it!

Exercise 38

MY SELF-MANAGED DEVELOPMENT ACTION PLAN

Using one of the action plans printed in this section (or take a blank sheet of paper and design your own) review the objectives you set yourself in Exercise 34 and select the objective, or the area in which you wish to focus and draw up your action plan.

You are now off and running – we hope! One final aspect of an action plan is the progress review. This should be built into each of your action plans, as it enables you to step back and take stock, reviewing how well or badly you are doing with the possibility of replanning, should this be necessary. As you all know, no matter how well you plan, things can go wrong, plans may alter, people change, etc. So we need to consider how we can plan for these contingencies or indeed how we can prepare our coping strategies in case things go wrong.

CONTINGENCY PLANNING

Life is never as straightforward as we expect it to be, so no matter how detailed and involved our thoughts and plans it is likely that they will change. These changes are not always for the worse. Indeed, often changes can be for the better, sometimes even offering us new options or opportunities. However, changes are not always welcome and for the better, for many of us we experience change as threatening and off-putting. As a means of ensuring maximum benefit from those positive diversions, minimizing the stress caused by unwanted changes, we feel that contingency planning is useful.

So what kind of diversions might we meet? It might be worth reflecting back to some of the earlier exercises in the book – in particular 'Serendipity' (p.119), 'My most significant learning experiences' (p.121), and 'Segmenting my learning' (p.122) – and thinking through some of the processes you went through in completing them. Take yourself back in time and think about what, how, when and why you learned, and who was involved in the learning process with you. Consider what diversions or hiccups you met with along the way. For instance:

- Was the timing of your original plan realistic?
- Did you find that you needed to involve more people in your learning network than originally planned?
- Did you have difficulties obtaining the necessary resources?
- Were you faced with challenges that you regarded as insurmountable?
- Did making mistakes throw you off course?
- Did you decide that your original objectives were unclear?

These are perhaps some of the more common diversions. For many of us there may be more personal ones that we meet. In thinking through these previous learning experiences it is useful to look for any repetitive patterns that emerge. Should you find any repetition then your contingency planning can take this into account.

If you build contingency planning into your self-managed development then the concept of developing options will become automatic for you. To us, options are important in order not only to deal with diversions but to give choice and flexibility. They can be regarded as being a bit like a roundabout or crossroads, that is, they provide you with alternative routes to enable you to reach your destination perhaps by a less direct route than originally planned.

Possibly one of the simplest and most straightforward approaches to contingency planning is to build in regular review times. This involves a very simple process of asking yourself a set of questions. You can of course develop your own questions; however, the ones we find particularly effective are:

- What is going well?
- What is going badly?
- What have I learned so far from this developmental experience?
- What do I want to do differently from now on?
- Am I experiencing any blockages that I have to deal with?

One regular blockage area or important reason for contingency planning that affects many of us is 'fear of failure' or 'the inability to learn from our mistakes'. It is worth considering that this whole area may actually involve elements of the self-fulfilling prophecy that having failed at something once you will never be able to master it! For instance, people say, 'I was no good at Mathematics at school so I will never understand the finances of a company' or 'I failed my O Level at school so I will never be able to learn a foreign language!'. However, as Mary Pickford, the actress, once said: 'If you have made mistakes … there is always another chance for you … you may have a fresh start any moment you choose, for this thing we call "failure" is not the falling down, but the staying down'. Or indeed, to quote Michael Korda, 'The freedom to fail is vital if you are going to succeed. Most successful people fail time and time again, and it is a measure of their strength that failure merely propels them into some new attempt at success'.

I suppose the message here is the old adage 'If at first you don't succeed, then try, try again'.

There are no easy or magic answers to deal with this issue except perhaps having the willpower and commitment to take on such challenges in conjunction with the six Ps:

- proper
- prior
- planning
- prevents
- poor
- performance.

So, at its simplest, most diversions can be dealt with by simply having a good plan in place, doing thorough preparation to begin with and then building in staged reviews at specific points of time in the self-managed development process.

Other more complex diversions are almost certain to hit us from time to time. For instance:

- job changes
- redundancy
- people in our learning network coming into and going out of our lives
- house moves
- family changes.

All of these and many more are difficult to plan for. However, if you have done your planning and preparation and you do regular reviews, any disruption can be kept to a minimum and re-routeing should be a reasonably straightforward affair.

COPING STRATEGIES

Our coping strategies are the techniques we develop for dealing with disappointments and stress in our lives. Self-managed development, like other aspects of our life, is not going to be without stress and disappointment; so how do we cope?

 Exercise 39

MY COPING STRATEGIES

Think back over the past few years. Focus on any disappointments or stressful periods in your life and note down the techniques you used and the people who helped to get you through that time.

_____

_____

_____

_____

_____

_____

Examine your notes for any patterns that emerge. Ask yourself if there are specific approaches you use for dealing with stress? Are there certain people in your life who you turn to in times of stress? These are your coping strategies!

Other people, whoever they are, often provide you with the necessary support, advice or help. So, for many of you, someone (or possibly more than one person) in your learning network will be the person to whom you turn when something goes wrong or when you need to cope with a disappointment, diversion or mistake.

Other coping strategies that people tell us about include:

- taking time off to recharge your batteries
- giving yourself a treat
- replanning or rescheduling your goal
- re-examining your whole approach.

Whatever your coping strategies are it is important that you recognize them and use them when necessary. Dealing with stressful situations as they happen can save time and unnecessary effort in the long run. Managing your own development is a new opportunity and challenge for many people. Consequently, like most new experiences in life there will be ups and downs. The important thing is 'Always do your best. Because, what you plant now, you will harvest later' (O.G. Mandino).

KEEPING TRACK

Our plan in writing this book is to encourage you to take more responsibility for your own development and to put you in control. Many of us (or maybe most of us) like to be able to keep track not only of where we are going but also of where we have been. In the context of self-managed development this can prove useful in career- and life-planning. Indeed it is useful also to keep a record not only of our achievements but of the routes we take to get there. They may be helpful at some point in the future.

While this book is aimed at helping you to get started on the process of self-managed development the motivation for keeping it going has to come from you yourself. For some of you keeping track will simply be a memory process. But for others of you a more structured approach is required.

One technique we find quite useful for 'keeping track' is to develop a personal learning journal. At the least sophisticated level this can be a notebook or loose-leaf binder where you can collect your action plans and indeed add other notes of importance to yourself. At a more sophisticated level you could allocate a section of your Filofax to the topic of self-managed development and perhaps assign pages for action plans, progress reviews and important notes. For those of you with home computers you could even design a fully automated personal learning journal or even prepare yourself a personally designed one for inclusion in your Filofax.

Again whatever technique you decide to approach for keeping track of your self-managed development it must suit your own specific needs. One final exercise before you set off on your self-managed development journey that may well help to keep you on track or to bring you back on course if you have meandered off it is to write a letter to yourself.

 Exercise 40

LETTER TO MYSELF

Take a blank sheet of writing paper, and on it write today's date and compose a short letter to yourself. The contents should indicate what your action plan is and the timescale. Put the letter into a sealed envelope, address it to yourself, put a stamp on it, then give it to a trusted colleague or friend and ask your friend to post it to you in three months time (or some other time appropriate to you).

This acts not only as a reminder of 'good intentions' but also as a conscience jogger!

STAGE SUMMARY

This final part of our journey has:

- Asked you to focus on your self-managed development objectives.
- Introduced you to ways to plan and analyse your route
- Explored the concepts of contingency planning and coping strategies
- Suggested that you develop your own system for keeping track of your journey.

We hope you have enjoyed the journey so far. Our intention has always been to help you prepare yourself for the most demanding and yet exhilarating journey of all – the journey of life!

INDEX